CONCILIUM
Religion in the Seventies

CONCILIUM

EDITORIAL DIRECTORS:
BASIC EDITORIAL COMMITTEES: Roland Murphy and Bruce Vawter (Scripture) • Giuseppe Alberigo and Anton Weiler (Church History)
EDITORIAL COMMITTEES: *Group I: Christian Faith:* Edward Schillebeeckx and Bas van Iersel (Dogma) • Hans Küng and Walter Kasper (Ecumenism) • Johann Baptist Metz and Jean-Pierre Jossua (Fundamental Theology) *Group II: Christian Ethics:* Franz Böckle and Jacques-Marie Pohier (Moral Theology) • Christian Duquoc and Casiano Floristán (Spirituality) • Andrew Greeley and Gregory Baum (Sociology of Religion) *Group III: The Practical Church:* Alois Müller and Norbert Greinacher (Pastoral Theology) • Herman Schmidt and David Power (Liturgy) • Peter Huizing and William Bassett (Canon Law)
THEOLOGICAL ADVISERS: Juan Alfaro • Marie-Dominique Chenu • Yves Congar • Gustavo Gutiérrez Merino • René Laurentin • Karl Rahner • Roberto Tucci
LAY SPECIALIST ADVISERS: Luciano Caglioti • August-Wilhelm von Eiff • Paulo Freire • Jean Ladrière • Pedro Lain Entralgo • Paul Ricoeur • Barbara Ward Jackson • Harald Weinrich
EXECUTIVE SECRETARY: (Awaiting new appointment), Arksteestraat 3–5, Nijmegen, The Netherlands

New Series: Volume 9, Number 9: Spirituality

EDITORIAL BOARD: Christian Duquoc • Casiano Floristán • Hans Urs von Balthasar • Maurice Bellet • Albert-Marie Besnard • Ladislaus Boros • Johannes Bours • Bernard Bro • Pietro Brugnoli • Carlo Carozzo • Michel de Certeau • Paul Duployé • Juan Esquerda Bifet • Antonin van Galen • Michel de Goedt • Gustavo Gutiérrez Merino • Henricus Hendrikx • Marcel Henry • Hoàng-sy-Quý • Patrick Jacquemont • Eugene Kennedy • Ernest Larkin • Jean Leclercq • José Morán • Jan Peters • Federico Ruíz Salvador • Charles Schleck • Jean-François Six • Josef Südbrack • Frits Tillmans • James Walsh • Friedrich Wulf

SPIRITUAL REVIVALS

Edited by
Christian Duquoc and
Casiano Floristán

Herder and Herder

1973
HERDER AND HERDER NEW YORK
815 Second Avenue
New York 10017

ISBN: 0–8164–2573–6

Cum approbatione Ecclesiastica

Library of Congress Catalog Card Number: 73–6432

Printed in the United States

CONTENTS

Editorial

THERE are signs, both in the churches themselves and outside their immediate spheres of influence, that the forecasts made by the secularizing theologians have not been borne out in fact. These signs are often very difficult to assess, but their undoubted existence has prompted us to devote this issue of *Concilium* to "religious revival". This term refers to those movements in the churches and on their periphery which bear witness to the need for a quasi-mystical fervour if the Good News is to be heard.

We therefore asked a sociologist, D. Hervieu-Léger, to give an appraisal of the symptoms of a religious revival. Even if her diagnosis is not accepted by many readers because it is so severe, it certainly provides food for thought to those who think that the churches are close to overcoming their present crisis.

It is not, however, enough simply to consult sociologists in order to discern the working of the Spirit in society, since this is not primarily their function. We have to take Scripture as our norm and here R. Murphy examines Deuteronomy as a document of revival. Even during the Old Testament period there was monotony and as the people of Israel moved further and further away from the early stage of their history, the need to make that period present and actual became more urgent. This was the work of the Spirit of Yahweh.

We have also to discern that Spirit today. Are these revivals really signs of the presence of the Spirit and what direction is that Spirit taking? This question is examined by F. Urbina as far as Christianity is concerned and by J. M. Velasco in the case of non-Christian religions. G. Remmert looks at the connection between these revivals and political praxis.

It is not, however, sufficient to confine ourselves to articles supported by historical and sociological data. We have also to consider a number of contemporary religious revivals. This is why the bulletins in this issue are devoted, for example, to Pentecostalism and the "Word out of Silence" symposium in the United States, to the links between the freedom movements and religious revival in South America and to the changes taking place in the religious life today. The data provided and the socio-historical analyses made will enable the reader to judge for himself whether the authors' diagnoses are correct or not.

Some readers would probably have preferred us, as editorial directors, to state our opinion about the many different views expressed in this issue. This might have been possible without indicating the editors' preference for one article rather than for another, but the wiser course seemed to be to allow the reader to judge for himself by providing information about the very diverse interpretations made of this modern phenomenon.

The directors' opinion ought, in any case, to be clear enough from the fact itself that they have chosen to devote this issue of *Concilium* on "Spirituality" to this particular phenomenon. If they had been fanatically in favour of the modern process of secularization, for example, or preoccupied with charismatic renewal, they would not have chosen spiritual revival as the theme of this number. They believe that, whatever conclusion we may reach regarding their inner value, these movements undoubtedly reveal a serious absence of the mystical element today in the churches.

One aim of this issue, then, is to draw attention to this absence. Another is to provide information about these revivals. It is, after all, only by examining these revivals that the aims of this issue can be achieved. Finally, we are bound to conclude from the various contributions to this issue that the churches cannot simply behave as governments so often do during a crisis, and continue to deal with their ordinary, day to day business.

CHRISTIAN DUQUOC
CASIANO FLORISTÁN

PART I
ARTICLES

Danièle Hervieu-Léger

Signs of a Contemporary Religious Revival?

I. A Contradiction of the "Post-Christian Epoch"

"JESUS is coming back!" The slogan from the campuses and hippie communes of the West Coast of the United States is a flat retort to the equally famous slogan "God is dead!" which made the fortune of the theology of secularization, another trans-Atlantic product. The contrast is striking. On the one hand, there is the effort made by theologians to justify the disqualification of the Christian message in a social universe in which technological and scientific positivity destroys the credibility of any assertions of transcendence. On the other, we see religion coming back in force, effervescent, exuberant, shaking entire social groups. The critical and hermeneutical work practised in the churches for decades now seems to have been swept aside by the rigorous fundamentalism of these "new Christians". Religious emotion, bursting the bonds of orthodoxy, reasserts its rights against exegetical and theological refinements. The desire to recover the fervour of an idealized version of genuine primitive Christianity is a justification for keeping at a distance from the churches, whose "abdication" before the secularity of the world one understands as the form taken today by their historic compromises with profane society. The communion of believers shatters official boundaries and denominational frontiers. The hope of a new world ignores both political attempts to change society and the escapes offered to drug trippers and "sexplorers", and concentrates on waiting for and proclaiming the Kingdom. The echo, by hundreds of stickers on the walls of the Faculté de Vincennes, of the question "Jesus is coming back—are you ready?" shows that the movement has spread far from its North American home.

The extent of the phenomenon of the "Jesus Revolution" in the United States, the often spectacular character of its manifestations (such as the famous collective baptisms in the Pacific or the Boston paschal vigil of 1971) and its orchestration by the mass media were ideally suited to draw attention to a contradiction which is appearing in a watered-down form in most Western countries. Everywhere, though in varying degrees, the political, economic and intellectual influence of the churches is being weakened. The time is past when the rulings of religious authorities in matters of ethics, sex, politics, etc., determined individual and collective behaviour, not just within the immediate circle of the believing community, but in society as a whole. It is of course important not to overestimate the ideological grip exerted by religious organizations in the past, and it would be false to imagine a Christendom in which nothing and no one escaped the power of the Church. It is none the less true that the Church is tending everywhere to lose the ideological predominance (if not monopoly) which was shaken but not abolished by the Renaissance, the Enlightenment and then the beginnings of industrial capitalism.

However imperfect totals of practising Christians may be as a measure of changes in the vitality of religion, the decreasing numbers of the faithful show the weakness of the churches' language as a mobilizing force. In general at least, religious beliefs are no longer the decisive, "coagulating" element in the social consensus. It is becoming rare, if not exceptional, for church membership to be a primary factor in the social integration of individuals. Church membership is in this way gradually relegated to the area of private life in which the freedom left to the individual is proportional to the socially inoffensive character of its exercise.

Now at the same time that the tendency to the social decline of religion, as identified with the process of the social marginalization of traditional religious organizations, seems to be in operation everywhere, we are witnessing a contradictory outburst of religious fervour which is escaping from the institutional channels. Intense community experiments, more or less informal religious networks and interdenominational and even inter-religious fraternities are developing with a speed which has taken by surprise the leaders and faithful of the official churches. The representatives of the official churches have enough to do in adapting their pastoral and apostolic strategies to a cultural and social situation in which they rightly feel that religious evidence is being subjected to its most severe questioning yet.

The challenge to the churches provided by the "Jesus Revolution" is a question that is to a great extent avoided in Europe. Various excuses are made to minimize its importance: its folksy aspects, its specifically American character or even the commercial exploitation which is made of it are stressed. At most, it is treated as a symptom of a sick society, and the appearance of Jesus freaks in European countries is generally attributed to a process of imitation, and therefore dismissed.

But what of the informal groups, grass-roots communities, spontaneous groups, etc., which are multiplying on the fringe of the institutions and often in opposition to them? They are described alternately as a ground-swell which is Christianity's only chance and as a threat to the unity of the Church. In due course the very existence of the phenomenon will be questioned and treated as a myth produced by the collective consciousness of believers whose security has been destroyed by the crisis in their churches. There is the same ambivalence, the same contradictory assessments, of religious networks which increasingly escape from the control of the authorized religious organizations and even from that of their founders. What is it that brings hundreds of searching Christians to the abbey of Boquen with their demand for a new style of church communion? What is it that inspired the groups of young people connected with Taizé when they prepared their Council or assembled to a total of over 3,000 for a night of prayer last Unity Week in Paris? Explanations which rely on the effect of a charismatic leader at the centre of these movements or on the curiosity aroused by the focuses such as Boquen, Taizé, Sainte-Beaume, St Michel de Cuxa, etc., are quite inadequate to account for the social phenomenon of the religious migrations which take place around them. And any hypothesis would still have to explain even more diffuse phenomena which also reflect this unexpected and complex revival of religion. One of these is the growth of prayer groups among Christians who even a short while ago put their main emphasis on a more questioning search for their religious identity, to the extent of postponing to a later time any joint celebration.

As the artificial character of official groupings based on a postulated "religious consensus" capable of transcending the social differences between the faithful and their possible antagonisms was realized, the tendency grew to link collective expression of the faith to real and acknowledged solidarities among the participants, particularly in social and political questions. This has not been stopped by the present movement, but it now coexists with a tendency to emphasize the "lyrical and poetic" dimension of strictly religious celebrations in both small communities and larger movements. In these, spontaneity of expression is the rule, and attempts are made to free the verbal and musical expression of the faith from the restrictions of the standardized liturgies issued by the religious authorities. The desire to introduce bodily expression into celebrations in an effort to remove individual and collective inhibitions is common to groups which have different relations to the Church, different theological positions and different views of the social involvement appropriate to religious bodies. This desire nevertheless creates a relationship between communities as different as the Christian hippie communes of the United States, groups of critical young religious in Belgium or Germany or grass-roots student communities in France and Italy. In very different forms, the "celebration" is generally expected to try to manifest here and now among the participants the possibility of a reconciliation and a communion which is destined to include all mankind.

II. AN AMBIGUOUS REVIVAL

Reconciliation is sought in prayer and prefigured in the heat of euphoria which expresses and feeds the religious enthusiasm of these new Christians, rather than being won through partisan involvement in social struggles. Emphasis is restored to communion in the faith rather than to the social affinities of the members of religious groups. This simplicity of faith is vaunted against the hesitant sophistications of politicized Christian intellectuals. No wonder the churches tend to take a very positive attitude towards this apparent turning of the tide of opposition. Cardinal Daniélou's expressions of pleasure at the religious renaissance symbolized by the Jesus Revolution are particularly significant of the new hope of religious authorities which had been badly shaken by the upsurge of secularism. Apparently the "enthusiasts" are less sensitive than the "politicals" to the unequal character of the distribution of power in the churches, and their frequent refusal to join in any direct challenge to the system is cause for rejoicing among those who were beginning to worry at the extent of the anti-institutional movement explicitly opposing them. Very often even the use by church officials of the term "religious revival" means no more than "a waning of the opposition movement in the churches".

The sense in which those involved use the word "revival" to describe the fervour which animates them is, however, quite different. In their view the various manifestations of an upsurge in religious enthusiasm mark the end of a torpor which they attribute to the churches themselves. Some groups go no further than denouncing the prevalent inertia, bureaucratization and the clogging of the communications network in the churches. Others regard the collusion of the churches with the dominant social system and the values by which it supports itself as the source of their impotence to bear witness to the radicalism of the gospel. All of them call for the regeneration of a "prophetic" Christianity to restore the social dynamism stifled by the organization.

While a more "political" trend tried to direct the critique of the ideological imprisonment responsible for their social impotence into the churches themselves, more and more groups of fervent Christians deny either formally or in practice the possibility that institutions as such can be "converted" and link a rebirth of Christianity to the personal conversion of each believer. The Church can only be holy if each individual Christian is on the path to holiness. This attitude, like the importance given to the intensity of the personal experience of the faithful rather than their submission to a rule of faith or practice, puts these groups clearly into Troeltsch's category of the sect.

Are these "parallel Christians", with their own organizations on the fringes of the institutional churches, less of a protest against these institutions than those who want to undermine the clerical monopoly of authority or change the direction of the churches' intervention in society? Nothing is less certain. Is the fundamentalism (in some cases) of the first more easily absorbed by the churches' systems of ideological regulation than the progressive theology of the second? It is doubtful. To seek a confrontation implies recognition of the adversary. The very tolerance of these "grace groups" for religious institutions in one sense is a sign of the little importance they attach to them. In many ways, indifference is the most radical form of opposition, and in this respect many of the groups of new Christians fit into a permanent movement in the history of Christianity which, under the banner of "no contact", expresses a radical rejection of the reality **thu**s denied.

Rejection of the churches and religious authorities is not, however, automatically connected with opposition to the social order. The problem is to tell whether the non-ecclesial character of these groups is one side of an unworldliness which includes a general social protest. If it is, we have to try to understand what social and ideological processes are produced by this social extension of political opposition and what it reveals of the power of the dominant system to keep to its fringes the social effects of the contradictions it produces. The instance of the small number of autarchic communities defined by their religious views is then to be understood against the background of not specifically religious phenomena which express a general "root and branch" attitude which includes even the forms of struggle against the system which is rejected.

It is also possible, however, that a religious rejection of the churches is the only point of impact of a critique of institutions. In this case it will no longer be a social extension of political opposition, but a spiritual one, and the "religious revival" will be the final mystification of the dominant system. By restricting the protest of youth to the religious sector, which is neutral to the ideological necessities of advanced capitalism, it will be able to secure an even stronger grip on all other sectors of social life.

The following of the hippie movement by the Jesus Revolution could be interpreted on these lines as a further stage in the American system's recovery of control of the protest of its youth. The geographical and social localization of opposition within small groups experimenting with a different model of society on the edge of social life was finally beginning to break down the logic of the social system at the level of the contradictions it produced (poverty, race, pollution, etc.). The ideological localization of protest reduces what might have been subversive (as a "cry", an appeal for a totally different society) in forms of social abstention which could have caught on. Religious illumination less frequently produces a strike against the dominant society than renewed submissiveness to the ethical norms of that society, especially in the sexual code it encourages.

The extreme example of America should not lead us to ignore the spread of the phenomenon to other Western countries. The question we have asked is whether the "religious revival" is not, in some aspects, the exploitation by the dominant system of ideological potential brought into being by the process of secularization which the system itself creates and controls. To the extent that advanced capitalism can maintain itself without the help of religion, we are witnessing the social marginalization of religious bodies which have become unneeded or even suspect as props of the social system and the religious dramatization of a social protest which is thereby emasculated because it is restricted to the sphere of ideology.

It should be remembered that the process has more than one implication. There can be no doubt that the evangelical radicalism developed in some, at least, of the movements in the religious revival may equally provide a language and a basis of collective expression for a social protest which is still unformed. The movement in itself is neither radical nor reactionary. It is fundamentally ambivalent, and capable of producing contradictory effects. The very fact, however, that it has developed to the greatest extent where the process of secularization has gone furthest raises a problem. Instead of being the point at which a religious protest and a social protest intersect and fertilize each other, as many such revivals in history have been, is not the present religious revival tending rather to dissociate the two so that both are easier to crush? There are outbursts of religion which could very well mean the end of Christianity, whatever their theological credentials. On this last point the sociologist, respectful of the proper limits of his discipline (in order to preserve the social recognition given to the "scientific" status of his language) will not risk a pronouncement. The question, however, remains, and is illustrated by an examination of a particular example within this complex and contradictory movement of religious revival, that of the Christian students in France. We shall now look at this as a way of trying to avoid the superficialities of general approaches.

III. Winning back Religion from Politics?

Less than two years ago a tendency began to appear among the students associated with the French Centres Catholiques Universitaires to give priority to forms of grouping which stressed common prayer, silent meditation on Scripture and the sharing of personal experience in the form of sharing in the gospel. The frenzied political activity of 1968–1970, in which young Christians went over in a body to a discovery of the political implications of fraternal love, seemed to have been replaced by a new phase of religious fervour. This happened in spite of the students' discovery, from political action itself, that no religious premise was necessary to give a reason, energy or direction to a general attempt to change society.

The Christian students who came into politics in May 1968 were very ready to transfer their hope of the Kingdom into the achievement of social utopia in micro-communities. Religious criticism of an unjust social order (an obstacle to the coming of the Kingdom) led into political criticism of the dominant system. This in its turn produced a political critique of the Church, as a willing and important factor in the maintenance of this rejected social system. "Political" grass-roots communities were often set up (with varying degrees of radicalism) in a desire to anticipate a different model of society whose establishment on a full scale had for the moment to be left to the future because of the absence of any mass movement to support it. In cases in which the religious basis of the groups was explicitly maintained part of the experiment with an alternative model of society was the development of an alternative model of the Church, and in particular of relations between clergy and laity. The members of these groups often regarded the overthrow by a revolutionary process of the dominant system as a necessary preliminary to the establishment of a church communion truly faithful to the gospel inspiration which dominated the life of the primitive Christian community. It was not uncommon among these new Christians for their aspiration for the eschatological appearance of a reconciled humanity to be based both on the dream-memory of the ideal and idealized community of the Acts of the Apostles and at the same time on a political analysis of the potential of the revolutionary movement. Their political commitment too, while explicitly directed towards the building of socialism, often continued to make use of the religious idea of the coming of the new man. The way to the kingdom of God was the freeing of the exploited, but the building of socialism required the birth of new, changed man, who was open to universal love.

"The rule of God is humanity learning to free itself from its multiple slaveries to become capable of real love, of sharing in the same spirit to the point at which all men together make one." This quotation from Bernard Besret[1] situates very well this meeting between history and saving history. Their interpenetration at the level of collective representations may perhaps be seen in the explicit coexistence in the language of the activists of religious themes of waiting and political themes of opposition. Even where the explicitly religious reference to another world was completely absorbed by the political demand for a changed society, the political language of these Christians and their ways of involvement in social struggles continued to bear traces of the religious antecedents of the utopia which underlay them.

The phenomenon is hardly surprising if we recall, with Henri Desroche, that utopia and hope are "twin sisters". "Utopia", Desroche says, "includes the hope for a different society. Hope includes the utopian vision of a different world. The strategy of both is based on otherness. Between the two the gap is narrow; utopian society has its religious trances and the world of hope has its earthly implications ('on earth as it is in heaven')."[2]

[1] Bernard Besret, Clés pour une Nouvelle Église (Paris, 1971), p. 73.
[2] Henri Desroche, Sociologie de l'Espérance (Paris, 1973), p. 37.

This remark can serve as a guide in tracing some current ideological shifts from "religion" to "politics", but it can equally help us to understand the still more recent tendency to a revival of religion. It may be noted in passing that the religious revival has not ended the process of political radicalization among Christian groups. This is still growing in the Churches, on their edges and often in opposition to them. And if, for some individuals or groups, the "return to religion" may be a stage of development following on an earlier phase of exclusive concentration on politics, a general tendency can be seen for the two activities to be pursued in parallel. In this respect the case of the Christian students of France is significant; it is used as an example here because the author can rely on first-hand information. In some groups formed in May 1968 or immediately after there could be seen a revival of interest in religion following directly on a burst of political energy which for a time had pushed aside all reference to any specifically Christian role.

To all appearances it was as though the weakening of the prospects for general change in society, connected with the recovery of control by the dominant system, had made a new space for religion in the lives of the activists. Strictly speaking, however, it would probably be too much to say that the failure of the revolution was the source of the expectation of a messianic intervention in history. The Christian militants of May 1968 had often come up through Catholic Action and been made open to revolutionary radicalism by a religious formation which made them aware of their duty to build the kingdom as part of their responsibility as Christians for the salvation of their brothers. To this extent, when political militancy fell back into routine they did not just return to previous religious positions, using them as a mere support for their utopian vision in a period of political inactivity.

It is nevertheless quite common for political communities with Christian roots (both among students and elsewhere) to undertake, after a period of religious latency of varying length, a more or less formal collective reflection on the relation between faith and politics, on the possibility of a political interpretation of the gospel or the kinds of social activity open to a transformed church community. It may be said that there is nothing original in this.

This may be so, but here the order of the questions normal in established religious groups is reversed and the possibility of a common inquiry into or expression of religion is based on the existence of a political consensus among the members of the community. No longer is it in the name of a common religious adherence that the group comes together to work out collectively the form of a Christian social praxis. It is a community of political interest and action which legitimates a collective inquiry into the possible function of the Christian faith as a critical tribunal on secular praxis. Political regulation of theological and ecclesiastical inquiry has become more important than religious regulation of social behaviour.

This means also that the movement very largely escapes from the direct control of ecclesiastical institutions, and usually totally from their ideological grip; one sign of the strength of this grip is the difficulty experienced very often by these groups in re-inventing religious language or redefining the ministries necessary to the life of the group without reabsorbing the unequal clerical-lay relation or reproducing the hierarchical structure of the dominant religious system. However, the extent of the elements carried over from the doctrine and practice of the churches is not the only measure of the size of the breach made in the churches' system of norms. Such groups form spontaneously and are not created by the church authorities. They lay down for themselves the social conditions for participation in their strictly religious activity, and channel the political experience of their members into their collective religious acts, if only, on a very modest scale, to provide intentions for group prayer or material to stimulate the sharing or exchange which takes the place of the sermon. All these features put the groups outside the range of external hierarchical control. As Jean Séguy says in this connection in a study of the internal dynamics of informal groups, "The locus of authority shifts from the minister to the assembly, whatever view is held of the theoretical relations between the two or of the nature of sacraments. At least implicitly, this challenges the boundaries of the Church, since political participation is regarded by many informal groups as the basis of Christian faith. This means that in these groups only those who correspond to the group's socio-religious norms can take part in the eucharist. Consciously or not each group regards itself as the Church and accepts the right to determine its limits and the norms of Christian life; authority rests with the assembly."[3]

An analysis of this shift in the locus of authority within the informal groups should be food for thought for those people in the churches who see the spiritual renewal in these groups as a sign that after a temporary thrashing about in politics these activists are rediscovering what the faith is really about. This view goes with the assumption that the groups are returning to the church institutions which their critics regard as the only social area within which religion can function. The new growth of religious activity does not, however, mean the end of this shift of authority, but rather strengthens it.

It is certainly quite often true that the process of going back to religion is accompanied by a weakening of collective determination to expose the contradictions of religious institutions which are regarded as repressive and reactionary forces. This fact is a comfort in assessing the situation for those who see the aggressiveness towards the Church of the Christian militants who came so recently into politics as no more than a short-lived fever, a mere transposition into religion of a general and typically adolescent challenge to authority.

There is no point in stressing the reductionist and ideological character of this interpretation of the anti-institutional upsurge inside and outside the Church. There can be no doubt, however, that the political challenge to the operation of religious institutions is also a struggle for the redistribution of political power in the churches which automatically accepts their existence and social importance.

In many cases maturity and political radicalization bring groups to a total indifference with regard to the official religious bodies. They see the Church as a secondary front, and other, more crucial struggles have first call on their energy as militants. On the other hand, religious revivals in grass-roots communities often have the same effect. For most of the time they give rise to an evangelical radicalism by which these groups justify their choice of a way of life which breaks with the norms of the dominant

[3] Jean Séguy, *Les Groupes informels dans l'Église* (Strasbourg, 1971).

society, by reducing their needs to consume, voluntarily limiting their standard of living, and sometimes forming self-sufficient economic units with no connection (or only minimal connections) with the productive system, and so on. Within the communities formed on this basis (which are not numerous), emphasis is placed on the quality of personal relations and the intensity of communication between the members. In the strictly religious sphere, the call for sharing grows stronger, and pushes into second place the question of what relations, if any, should be kept with the churches. For example, if all or most of the religious functions which in the official groups are generally monopolized by the clergy are transferred to the group as a whole, group members more often justify this by the demands of their collective religious experience than by the need for some sort of demonstration of ecclesial democracy in the face of the institutions. It is nevertheless true that if one goes beyond the language of their members, these groups which are indifferent to the churches are in fact focuses of subversion in the dominant religious system. Their sociological significance is close to that of sects in other historical periods in that, with or without theological arguments, they give priority to the spirit over orthodoxy, to charisms over the institution and to personal illumination over regulated adherence to a body of doctrine. This indicates how far they are from being the churches' outposts in a religious reconquest of secular society with an exploratory function which might sooner or later give way to reforms initiated and controlled by the churches.

If, however, one follows the definition of the phenomenon of sects given by Ernst Troeltsch, can it be said that the groups affected by this religious revival show the indifference to the culture and political life of their time which is a feature of sects? Evangelical radicalism sometimes takes the place of the social radicalism which it may itself have created at a previous stage. But just as often it combines with it as the basis of the utopia of a transformed world in collective representations, of the specific point at which Coeurderoy says "the insurrection of desire and the insurrection of the masses join".

It is not uncommon for a return of religious activity to be accompanied by a retreat from all forms of militant action in politics as such. It can be an alibi for those whose revolutionary commit-ment was never more than a projection of their religious phantasms and not the expression of a class solidarity. This is in any case hardly surprising when one bears in mind the social groups in which this movement most often develops, students, teachers, intellectuals, petty bourgeois generally, whose political radicalization, depending as it does on the increased precarious-ness of their social status, has difficulty in escaping from the sphere of ideological choices. The position is less clear than in the case of the Jesus Revolution, which gives individual conversion higher priority than any mass action directed against the social system and even criticizes the churches for their desire to inter-vene in social and political life on the ground that it distracts them from their spiritual mission. Nevertheless, the tendency exists.

Subversion at one remove is the answer of those who believe in the social force of the movement, who claim that a change of heart necessarily produces a new social praxis. The evangelical ideal adopted by the new Christians who condemn the reign of money is an implicit condemnation of the hypocrisy of Western liberal humanism, and attacks the ideological foundations of capitalist society. Nevertheless, if there is a protest, it is primarily ideological and offers no challenge to the social and economic system which produces both the collective ideals which are least challenged and their contraries. (The toleration of the dominant system in the United States for the Jesus Revolution is significant in this connection.)

Every religious revival is, from the point of view of its social repercussions, fundamentally ambivalent. Even if religion is, in Gramsci's term, a "generalized utopia" and as such has a "poli-tical value", any reactivation of religious fervour which expresses hope for a totally different world still does not automatically re-lease forces capable of changing the social system. The history of religious revivals provides plenty of evidence for this ambivalent character of religious hope which Henri Desroches, in his *Socio-logie de l'Espérance*, summed up in his distinction between "in-hibiting" and "inspiring" expectation. It is beyond the scope of this article to discuss the particular conditions, depending on the social position of the bearer group and the social dynamics of the particular society of which it is a part, in which expectation can be inhibiting or instead be motivating and inspire a social struggle, or the ways in which it can change direction from inhibiting to mobilizing.

It is nevertheless clear that in the case of the present movement in its various forms the ambivalence characteristic of religious turbulence is increased by an ambiguity deriving from features of the social and cultural environment in which it has developed. The present movement has grown, not in a phase of extension of the social control of religious institutions, but amid a weakening of their ideological, political and economic influence. Consequently protest against the churches' tolerance of the world no longer necessarily involves an implicit or explicit protest against the dominant social order which turns either into a break with the world or into demands on or revolt against society. It is not even clear whether this religious renewal of utopian ideas in a secularized world "creates creativity", to use Henri Desroche's phrase, or whether it is a sign of the failure of social utopias and the exhaustion of all political will for social change in the face of the formidable capacity of the dominant system to absorb all opposition. This would leave as the only alternative the worsening of the contradictions produced by the system until they demystify the class struggle and regenerate the revolutionary force of a mass movement.

Translated by Francis McDonagh

Roland Murphy

Deuteronomy—A Document of Revival

THE history of Israel mirrors the fidelity and the infidelity of the people of God. It is not difficult to underline the infidelity; the prophets were particularly adept at that, and Israel was generous enough to preserve this unhappy record. But we know that in the case of many prophets there was also some kind of revitalizing of religion. Hence Isaiah can speak of his disciples (8. 16), and an Isaian school seems ultimately to have been responsible for the oracles attributed to him in Isa. 40–66. For most of the prophets we are forced to postulate some faithful group that would have listened to and preserved the message. But we are deliberately setting aside the prophetic movement, which did produce both renewal and revival in various quarters, in order to concentrate on one document that had a chequered history in terms of its various editions, but which always remained a document of reform and revival—the Book of Deuteronomy.

I. THE MEANINGS OF DEUTERONOMY

At first sight, a literary text is not a promising beginning for an insight into a spiritual awakening. But Deuteronomy is an extraordinary composition that reflects several critical periods in the life of the people. It was originally conceived in the monarchical period in the Northern Kingdom of Israel, it emerged as "the Book of the Law" (2 Kings 22. 8) in 621 in Judah and it was finally edited in the crucial times of the Exile (587–539). We want to illustrate reform and revival within Israel on the basis of

the Deuteronomic tradition which refused to die and which became a pillar of Judaism and the New Testament itself. The
formation of the book itself suggests three levels of interpretation[1]
and at each level we are confronted with revival.

1. Most of the work grew up in the pre-exilic period, and in
the atmosphere of the cultic renewal of the covenant. There are
many passages that bear the imprint of their liturgical origins—a
revival is going on. On this level every reader is caught up by the
hortatory style that characterizes 5–30: "Hear, O Israel! The
Lord our God is one Lord; and you shall love the Lord your God
with all your heart, and with all your soul, and with all your
might. And these words which I command you this day shall be
upon your heart; and you shall teach them diligently to your
children, and you shall talk of them when you sit in your house,
and when you walk by the way, and when you lie down, and
when you rise. And you shall bind them as a sign upon your
hand, and they shall be as frontlets between your eyes. And you
shall write them on the doorposts of your house and on your
gates" (Deut. 6. 4–9).

For the most part, the dry language of law is transformed, even
in the celebrated Deuteronomic law code (chs. 12–26); now the
Law is preached: "You are sons of the Lord your God; you shall
not cut yourselves or make any baldness on your foreheads for
the dead. For you are a people holy to the Lord your God, and
the Lord has chosen you to be a people for his own possession,
out of all the peoples that are on the face of the earth" (Deut.
14. 1–2).

Thus the Deuteronomic revival cajoled and persuaded. Its
primary call was to the love of God—this was the great commandment (cf. Mk. 12. 29), and it was expressed in several idioms
(cf. Deut. 10. 12)—Israel was to hear the Lord's commands, to
fear him, to walk in his ways, to serve him, to cling to him,
to swear by his name, to observe his commandments. The Lord's
saving deeds were put forth as motives for Israel's fidelity: the
choice of the patriarchs (10. 15), the deliverance from Egypt
(11. 2–4), the gift of the land (11. 10–12).

But the terms of the covenant with Yahweh were also enjoined

[1] N. Lohfink, *Höre, Israel!* (Düsseldorf, 1965).

under threat. The blessing/curse formula that characterized the Hittite vassal treaties of the ancient Near East lies behind the pungent idiom that a sedentary agrarian people could understand: "And if you will obey my commandments which I command you this day, to love the Lord your God, and to serve him with all your heart and with all your soul, he will give the rain for your land in its season, the early rain and the later rain, that you may gather in your grain and your wine and your oil.... Take heed lest your heart be deceived, and you turn aside and serve other gods and worship them, and the anger of the Lord be kindled against you, and he shut up the heavens, so that there be no rain, and the land yield no fruit, and you perish quickly off the good land which the Lord gives you" (Deut. 11. 13–17; cf. Deut. 27–28).

Gerhard von Rad first pointed out the central role of the confession in Deut. 26. 1–11.[2] By means of the liturgy described in this passage, Israel tied in the present with the past; the first fruits of the land were to be returned to the Lord who had done such wondrous things for his people. The "recall" of the past is reflected in the constant command to *remember*: "And you shall remember all the way which the Lord your God has led you these forty years in the wilderness" (Deut. 8. 12). "You shall remember the Lord your God for it is he who gives you power to get wealth..." (8. 18). This reminder alternates with the warning, "not to forget"; "Take heed lest you forget the Lord your God... (8. 11; cf. 8. 19).

These soundings in Deuteronomy still convey across the years the insistent demands of the essence of Deuteronomic preaching, the summons to love the Lord. It has been conjectured (G. von Rad), and accepted by many (R. de Raux), that this was the fruit of the preaching of the Levites. Be that as it may, one cannot fail to see the liturgical framework in which this summons was placed. The constant "today", the liturgical "now", rings out as Israel wiped away time and identified herself with the fathers who entered into the covenant at Horeb. Paradoxically, it was not with the fathers that the covenant was made—"but with us,

[2] J. Schreiner, "The Development of the Israelite 'Credo'," *Concilium*, Dec. 1966 (American edn., Vol. 20).

who are all of us alive here this day" (Deut. 5. 3). In fact, all Israel was present in those remote Horeb events: "On the day that you stood before the Lord your God at Horeb... You came near and stood at the foot of the mountain... Then the Lord spoke to you..." (4. 10–12). Every succeeding generation heard these words and all were transported back into the Mosaic covenant experience by the liturgical re-enactment which gave rise to the words in the biblical text.

2. Deuteronomy can be read also from another point of view— within the framework of the so-called Deuteronomic history: Jos., Judges, 1–2 Sam., and 1–2 Kings). This history had as its original introduction (according to M. Noth), Deut. 1. 1–4. 43, before Deut. 4. 44–30. 20 was inserted. Seven centuries of Israelite history were unified according to the Deuteronomic viewpoint: fidelity to the Lord means prosperity; infidelity brings disaster (Deut. 11. 26–32; Judges 2. 11–23). Thus the catastrophe of the destruction of Jerusalem in 587 was explained.

Now when one looks back at the sermons of Moses which give structure to the book (1. 4–4. 43; 4. 44–28. 69; 29. 1–30. 20) there appears what N. Lohfink has called a "morning freshness" about the work. The situation is calm—after the Exodus and before the Conquest. Israel is in the fields of Moab, poised for the crossing over the Jordan. This was the moment of possibility; the future opened before the People of God, and the Mosaic discourses laid out the hopeful programme: "Choose life, that you and your descendants may live, loving the Lord your God, obeying his voice, and cleaving to him; for that means life to you and length of days, that you may dwell in the land which the Lord swore to your fathers, to Abraham, to Isaac, and to Jacob, to give them" (Deut. 30. 19–20).

There is no escape from the poignancy of these words for a later generation—the "what might have been" in Israel's history. But such is the power of this book that succeeding generations heard words of hope, not despair, as G. von Rad has noted:[3] "Would anyone be surprised if Deuteronomy, after such religious decay, had simply considered Israel to be lost and a return to God

---

[3] G. von Rad, "Ancient Word and Living Word", *Interpretation*, 15 (1961), 3–13, p. 8.

to be impossible? But the opposite is the case. Deuteronomy erases seven centuries of disobedience and thoughtless ingratitude, places Israel once more in the desert before God, and lets Israel hear again the gracious election to be the people of the Lord's possession. This Israel experiences with no reduction the same thing now as before in the desert, and yet this Israel was not at all still the same. The Israel which Deuteronomy confronts had superficially hardly a point of resemblance to that people which once stood at the foot of Mount Sinai. Culturally and economically and politically it lived in very different conditions. But this is what we find so important about Deuteronomy, that it was able to speak the old gospel word of God's election undiminished in a situation which was so very different from that of old Israel."

3. Still another perspective emerges when one sees what finally became of the Book of Deuteronomy. During the exile it was joined to the first four books to form the Torah, or Law. The process of canonization of the sacred literature was now in full swing; the structure of Law, Prophets and Writings (the Tanak) was beginning to appear.

But the position of Deuteronomy is an unusual one. As J. A. Sanders has pointed out,[4] the Torah breaks the natural story line that goes from the Exodus and desert happenings into the Conquest (Joshua). By the insertion of Deuteronomy as the final book of the Pentateuch, these books are locked off from the story of Joshua and the Conquest which is their natural complement. What is the significance of this?

Put very bluntly, it was the triumph of Mosaic theology for Judah. The emphasis shifted from David to Moses. The primary authority was now derived from the time before the conquest (and not from the Davidic line in Jerusalem). As Sanders had indicated, Deuteronomy is the keystone in the formation of the Law, which "defined forever all Jewry as Judaism". We can see the power of Deuteronomy for the revival of the exiled people: "In Babylonia after the news had arrived in 586 B.C. that Jerusalem had fallen and the Temple had been destroyed, some elders went to the prophet Ezekiel and asked him the pertinent ques-

---

[4] J. A. Sanders, *Torah and Canon* (Philadelphia, 1972).

tion: "*Ek nihyeh?* How shall we live? In what now does our existence obtain? What now is our identity? The answer came in the form of the Pentateuch and the laws which JEDP had inserted within it. And that was when we knew that our true identity, the Torah par excellence, included the conquest neither of Canaan (Joshua) nor of Jerusalem (David) but that Sinai, which we never possessed, was that which we would never lose" (Sanders, p. 53).

Thus it is due to Deuteronomic influence that the Mosaic tradition became the basis of the Judaism that emerged with the exile. The structure of the three Mosaic discourses in the book give it the aura of a departure ceremony. The man who was the instrument of Israel's deliverance, the receiver of the Law, the guide during her forty years in the desert, is about to leave his people. He may not enter the Promised Land. He presents his last will and testament, as it were, before dying on Mt. Nebo. If there is an accent of sadness, even tragedy, in reading his final directions for his people, there is the hope and vision that at least *they* shall enter the Promised Land; Ezekiel's vision (ch. 37) of the dry bones arising out of the valley of death became a reality, thanks to the revival spearheaded by the Torah and the Deuteronomists.

II. The Deuteronomic Reform of Josiah

Thus far we have been considering Deuteronomy as revival literature. In addition to the revivalism of the liturgical renewals that have left their imprint on the text, is there a specific period of history that one can point to as the age of the Deuteronomic Reform? The reform of King Josiah (640–609) was based on Deuteronomy.

The discovery of "the book of the Law" in the eighteenth year of Josiah's reign (621 b.c.; cf. 2 Kings 22) is a turning-point in the history of Judah. The seventh century had been pretty much a disaster for Yahwism. Judah was practically a vassal state of Assyria, and political dependence involved religious dependence, as the long reign of Manasseh (687–642) shows. But Assyria entered on a decline that was to culminate in the fall of Nineveh in 612 to the neo-Babylonian forces. Politically, this gave Josiah the opportunity of asserting independence, even to the extent of exercising control over the territory of the former Northern Kingdom of Israel. His religious reform was thoroughgoing and based upon the programme afforded by Deuteronomy. All would agree that "the book of the Law" discovered in the Temple was some form of the Book of Deuteronomy, at least chs. 12–26. The writer of 2 Kings made this discovery the spearhead and symbol of the Josian Reform which actually had begun previous to the discovery itself (2 Chron. 34. 3). The reaction of King Josiah when Huldah the prophetess identified the book is in keeping with the threats laid down in Deut. 28. He tore his garments when he heard the document read aloud, and he proclaimed: "For great is the wrath of the Lord that has been kindled against us, because our fathers have not obeyed the words of this book, to do according to all that is written concerning us" (2 Kings 22. 13).

The concrete reforms which are described in 2 Kings 22–23 can be matched by the prescriptions of Deuteronomy. The abuses that had grown up in previous years were outlawed: necromancy (cf. Deut. 18. 11–12), the astral cult (cf. Deut. 17. 3), the prostitutes associated with the fertility rites (cf. Deut. 23. 18), the sacrifice of children to Moloch (cf. Deut. 18. 10).

The most typical reform was centralization of worship, in line with a constant Deuteronomic refrain, e.g., Deut. 12. 5–6: "You shall seek the place which the Lord your God will choose out of all your tribes to put his name and make his habitation, and thither you shall bring your burnt offerings and your sacrifices. . . ." Centralization of worship was a break with the ancient ways which permitted various local sanctuaries (Gilgal, Mizpah, Gibeon, etc.), while recognizing the central sanctuary of the Ark. But it was not a totally new move in Judah's traditions. A century before, King Hezekiah destroyed the local sanctuaries (2 Kings 18. 4), and had also applied this practice to what had been the Northern Kingdom (2 Chron. 30–31). In fact, this was used in the report of the Assyrian embassy outside the walls of Jerusalem (the siege of Sennacherib in 701), as an argument against Hezekiah (2 Kings 18. 22): How can Israel rely on Yahweh after Hezekiah has just suppressed his high places and altars? There seems to be no question, however, that this drastic move was a remedy against the syncretism (especially fertility rites) that characterized Israelite worship "on the high places". Although the Deuteronomic understanding of centralization probably referred originally to the Ark sanctuary (at Shechem), the application to the Jerusalem Temple in the South was a logical step. One may even see in it a reflection of Israel's belief that there was only one Yahweh—one Lord, one sanctuary.

With this emphasis upon centralization there emerged what has been called the "Name" theology. This represents the Deuteronomic effort to understand the mystery of the divine presence. Yahweh, of course, dwelt above the firmament in the heavenly temple. Then how was he present with his people? Through his Name. This view is far from the nominalism that we might attribute to it. The person is inseparable from his name; he is his name, according to Old Testament mentality. And the temple as the dwelling-place of Yahweh's name was a way of meeting the paradox of divine absence and presence, such as is reflected in the prayer of Solomon: "Will God indeed dwell on the earth? Behold, heaven and the highest heaven cannot contain thee; how much less this house which I have built! . . ." (1 Kings 8. 27). In Deuteronomy there is a constant refrain about the place where the Lord "puts" his name or causes his name to "dwell". This stands in contrast to the Priestly tradition which spoke of the divine *glory* which tabernacled or *tented* in the Temple. Both traditions are grappling with the inexpressible.

How is the Deuteronomic reform under King Josiah to be judged? Josiah himself came to a disastrous end in 609 when he tried to resist the forces of Pharaoh Neco, who was coming to the aid of the fading Assyrians. This unfavourable ending of a "good" king was a shock to the generally accepted view that the good were supposed to prosper. Moreover, the invective of Jeremiah against Judah and Jerusalem suggests that the Josiah reform had been only superficial. Scholars dispute about the role of this prophet in the reform itself. It is clear that he was active as a prophet early in the reign of Josiah, and it is likely that he supported it to a degree (H. H. Rowley). But in the last hectic twenty years of Judah's existence, he found himself forced to inveigh against certainties that were founded upon the Deuteronomic theology, such as the security that was "guaranteed" by the presence of the Lord in the Temple (Jer. 7. 3–15; 26. 1–9). From this point of view, the Deuteronomic reform under Josiah was short-lived. But as we have indicated above, the Book of Deuteronomy outlasts any failure. It is revival literature, and spills out beyond the time-conditioned character of a particular revival. The Josian reform, short-lived in fact, was only a part of the total reforming which the Book of Deuteronomy (in its several editions) sparked. If Deuteronomy did not ensure a conversion at the end of the seventh century (and what book can, in any century?), it had already given a message that was heard by more than one generation before this, and it was to live on in Israel's tradition to play a vivifying role.

III. The Later History of Deuteronomy

The *Nachleben*, or after-life, of Deuteronomy deserves particular emphasis. As R. E. Brown has remarked,[5] "Indeed, it is not too much to say that the religious spirit of observance inculcated by Deuteronomy and the Deuteronomic History enabled Yahwism to survive the exile." As we have seen, it is probable that the book assumed its final form during the critical period of the exile. And as the book was read and pondered in the post-exilic era, it assumed an eschatological character, and thus continued its work of re-vivifying Israel. A faithful Israel was understood as ever redeemable by the "God of the Fathers". There *would* be another prophet like Moses (Deut. 18. 15)—not a line of prophetical interpreters such as Isaiah or Jeremiah—but a prophet of the eschaton, or final period, who would, like Moses, lead his people back into loyalty, peace and joy.

A most interesting example of this after-life of the Book of Deuteronomy is to be found in the attitude of the so-called Essenes at the turn of the Christian era. This group of Jews retired to the desert of Judah in the second century B.C., and one of their primary foundations is the "monastery" discovered and excavated in the last twenty years. Many biblical and non-biblical manuscripts from the Qumran caves on the north-west shore of the Dead Sea illustrate this revival group. The emphasis on the covenant, so typical of Deuteronomy, is a characteristic of this

[5] R. E. Brown, *Deuteronomy* (Collegeville, 1965), p. 11.

people that called itself "the community of the Everlasting Covenant". In their "Manual of Discipline" (1QS 1. 16) it is specified that "all who embrace the Community Rule shall enter into the covenant before God". Every year there was a covenant renewal ceremony, with the characteristically Deuteronomic curses and blessings (1QS 1.18 ff.). The division of the tribes of Israel into thousands, hundreds, fifties and tens (Deut. 1. 15) formed a basis for the organization of the Qumran community which looked back to the desert generation for its ideal. The final "holy war" of the community was patterned after the doom war described in Deuteronomy. Deuteronomy is quoted by the priest who addresses the stalwarts of Qumran in the final battle: "Hear, O Israel, you draw near this day to battle against your enemies: let not your heart faint; do not fear, or tremble, or be in dread of them; for the Lord your God is he that goes with you, to fight for you against your enemies, to give you the victory" (Deut. 20. 3–4; 1QM 10. 3). More than fourteen manuscripts (fragmentary) of Deuteronomy are among the cache of biblical texts yielded by the eleven caves excavated in the vicinity of Khirbet Qumran.

The same telling influence of Deuteronomy is to be seen in the New Testament also where it is quoted more than eighty times. The great commandment (Deut. 6. 5) forms the basis of the Johannine emphasis on love (Jn. 13–15), which is the "new commandment" of Jesus (Jn. 13. 34). It is particularly significant that Jesus answers the devil at the temptation in the desert (Lk. 4. 1–13) with quotations from Deut. (8. 3; 6. 13; 6. 16).

IV. Conclusions

1. In terms of our model, the Book of Deuteronomy, revival means that some elements in the old tradition come alive again and speak to the people of God. A New Song (Pss. 96. 1; 98. 1; Is. 42. 10) updates the past. Hence the Deuteronomic emphasis on remembering, and the effort to re-present the key events of the past (Deut. 5. 3; 29. 12; cf. the eucharistic memory in 1 Cor. 11. 25–27).

2. Although continuity with the past is an undercurrent in spiritual renewal, this is not merely re-hashing. The paradox of

Is. 43. 18–19 is applicable here. After recalling the saving events of the Exodus as a type of the new deliverance from the Babylonian exile, the prophet cries out: "Remember not the former things, nor consider the things of old. Behold, I am doing a new thing; now it springs forth, do you not perceive it?" The revival reflects the past—but it goes beyond it.

3. Finally, we may note that our biblical model of revival, Deuteronomy-style, is not as narrow or bookish as it might first appear. This particular book reflects the oral tradition (liturgical, homiletical, etc.) that fed into it. Moreover, the steady re-shaping and re-editing of the work itself was tied into various moments of revival in the history of a people.

Claude Gérest

Spiritual Movements and Ecclesial Institutions: An Historical Outline

I. Spiritual Movements as Manifestations of or Challenges to the Institution

THE history of the Christian churches is punctuated by spiritual movements. These movements do not, *ipso facto*, constitute a challenge, and some of them even take it upon themselves to set in motion, for the benefit of the community out of which they emerge, an evangelical dynamism which they insist they have received from their traditions. Their aim is to manifest the real nature of the institution. Others have adopted a more critical attitude; but whatever the case may be, the very existence of these movements, quite apart from the positions they adopt, is a condemnation of the lack of sinew in the life of the churches. At the very least they indicate that the latter are not everywhere places of spiritual encounter, since it has been necessary to find this place within them or alongside them. And when, as has happened so often in recent centuries, spiritual movements are referred to as reawakenings or "revivals" this must imply that the institution is paralysed, or dead, or, to say the least, asleep.

Spiritual movements are something quite different from a simple reform of the Church. The latter can be brought about by correcting abuses and reinforcing the "canons" of thought, law and practice, but the movement is concerned, in the first place, with the rediscovery, not of principles or rules, but of a new spiritual impetus. Its frequently observed opposition to "orthodoxy" is not merely accidental. Preservation of the accuracy of theological discourse and concentration on precision of formulas are, in fact, preoccupations which run the risk of extinguishing all desire for renewal in the Spirit. Thus, in the eighteenth century, to take a notable example, the pietistic fervour of Zizzendorf, and the Moravian Brethren came into greater conflict with the conservative dogmatism of the Lutheran "right" than with the audacity and "secularism" of theologians influenced by the Enlightenment.

1. *Characteristics of the Spiritual Movement*

"Spiritual" people have appeared in the churches in many different guises: monks, staretz, "pentecostalists", determined pioneers, revolutionary prophets, wise elders, who, all of them, have borne witness to the fact that Christianity is not primarily a sociological or ideological construct, but a source of inspiration and community.

The search for immediacy and experiential knowledge is the common feature of very diverse movements in very different ages. To Christians who are satisfied with a sociological faith, and with obedience to tradition, the "spirituals" suggest a return to the sources—and one thinks first of the scriptural sources. "Revivals" have always encouraged reading of and love for the Bible. Even before the invention of printing the twelfth-century *pauperes Christi* did a great deal to disseminate the text, divide it into sections and translate it. But even the Book itself has a mediatory function—beyond it, the "spiritual" man looks for the One who speaks in it. Putting it at its most extreme—and it is the extreme —his veneration for the "sacred" text is less than his desire to produce a new one from it, as Schleiermacher said of the "religious expert" in his famous discourses of 1799. To put it in a more general way, to words *about* God he prefers words that come *from* God; he cares more about inspired action than about the moral conclusions to be drawn from a given teaching. Before God he is a mystic (even if he dislikes that particular word, which may evoke, quite wrongly, a mere technique of the interior life), before men a prophet. Through his action or his "passion" he succeeds in manifesting so completely the indwelling presence of the Spirit that to some it will look like identification—and the churches in their moments of suspicion are only too ready to denounce the "pantheism" of the spirituals (thus Rome with respect to the "brethren of the free Spirit", the Rhenish mystics, the Andalusian *Illuminati* and others later recognized as saints, or Luther with respect to the Anabaptists). In more than one case the accusation could be shown to be justified but the possibility of self-defence was not entirely ruled out, since there is no dearth of scriptural texts attesting to the quasi-identity of the believer and the God who dwells within him.

The God of the "spiritual man" does not simply become present in the here and now of the experience—he comes and brings with him the prospect of a future. The spiritual person is the witness of this future, and so his attitude has something surprising—even disconcerting—about it. The standards of plain common sense or of a cut-and-dried morality have been left behind; the stereotyped image of sanctity abandoned. If the spiritual man has a contemplative bias, he will be more concerned with ecstasy, with the going out from self towards the One who comes —in moments of personal recollection or in the exaltation of shared experience—than by set devotional practices or rites. If he is more inclined to action, his aim will be to hasten the emergence of a new world and new liberty. Orientated towards the future, he is always one step ahead and many will fail to understand him, or only grasp his significance in retrospect. The Florentine revolution of Savonarola might look like the return to an anachronistic theocracy, and Bernanos like a reactionary. But past models can only account, later, for the material aspect of their works; their inspiration is spent at the time in an appeal for renewal of the times.

It is not a matter for indifference that the God who comes and gives himself in the immediacy of the present moment should be called the Spirit. The Spirit is the supreme manifestation of the Trinity as a mystery of exchange and ecstasy. Paul Tillich has said that God stands at a distance from himself in his Son and that in the Spirit he rediscovers his unity and that this was clearly a figurative way of speaking which reminds Christians that God is not an inert being, but the ground of all being. He who says "the Spirit" announces the communion in God himself, and then between God and every living being. Furthermore, for every Christian who has not lapsed into modalism, the Spirit is "another Paraclete", intimate with the Son who speaks of "that which is his" without ever becoming identified with him. It is to the Spirit that we have been entrusted since the Passover of Jesus. It is he who makes the gospel a living reality for us, inducing us to rediscover it for ourselves, not merely to repeat it. His unity with the Son, and yet his complete otherness, ensures that without being separated from him, we too are entirely free in our life of communion with Christ. He is the "milieu" of liberty in which we open ourselves to God. "And we all," says St Paul, "with unveiled faces, beholding the glory of the Lord, are being changed into his likeness from one degree of glory to another; for this comes from the Lord who is the Spirit" (2 Cor. 3. 18). The spiritual men of history have not necessarily had any clear or precise understanding of the relationships within the Trinity, but they have learned to rely on the Spirit to teach them how to be faithful in the spirit of the gospel, and how to make the light and freedom it brings an inner reality for themselves.

2. The Complex Relationship between Spiritual Movements and Ecclesial Institutions

In search of immediacy, orientated towards the future, jealous guardians of their liberty, the "spiritual" naturally have difficulty in adapting themselves to institutions and in gaining acceptance from them. The opposition between Church and prophet is such a commonplace theme today that there is no longer any need to illustrate it.

By institution we understand here that ensemble of recognized discourse, rites, sacraments, ministries and legislation which assures the community its permanent place in time and its social identity. Such a framework hardly favours freedom of movement and inspiration and, what is more, in the Church all reference to the past where the key events are located is continually brought forward as justification for the entire institutional construct. At the same time, faith seems to be buoyed up at every turn by intermediaries: we believe on the testimony of witnesses accredited by the Church, and according to formulas which it preserves and imposes. This network of mediating devices has the effect of stifling permanently all spiritual élan. Yet on the other hand, the institutional Church has of necessity to maintain political links with other institutions of this world, and this constitutes an inexhaustible source of conflict with the champions of spontaneity and prophetic protest. Attacks on the "post-Constantinian" Church did not begin only yesterday, but date from Arnold of Brescia and the anti-clerical Christians of the twelfth century.

A barrier to the outpouring of the Spirit—so seems the institution in any polemical perspective and this is not completely groundless. But one should not cling to this interpretation, for example, and ignore what the institution has to say about itself and its relation to spiritual realities. If it is difficult for the Church to describe itself purely and simply as the body of the Spirit (which is how Möhler saw it in 1820), it does possess an awareness and a grasp of the Spirit which is uniquely its own and which enters into its definition of itself. The Church, as we have already said, looks towards the past, since it is essential to it that it should refer back to the events of its foundation; but it should not forget that these events manifest an upsurge of the Spirit and need to acquire renewed meaning in continual pentecosts. The formulas of faith contained in the creeds cannot replace the spiritual quest, they simply guide it. The sacraments are nothing unless they give access to the mysteries they unveil. The ministries, through which, above all, the Church takes shape as a social body, are geared to spiritual edification (cf. 1 Cor. 12. 27; Eph. 4. 11). There are charisms to designate and sustain those "who preside" and those "who rule" as well as those "who prophesy".

It is neither the purpose nor the principal desire of authority to "stifle the Spirit". Its vocation is rather to help manifest his presence. The hierarchical structure of a church can even become instrumental in heralding the new times, if, in its midst, "the first become last and masters become servants". This evangelical reversal of the social order is scarcely ever achieved, I shall be told, except on paper. That is true; but it is sufficient for the present discussion that the ecclesiastical authority should be able to recognize itself as fully responding to its vocation in some particular episode of its history where the prophetic and the institutional coincide.

Instances of this are not entirely wanting—consider, for example, the resistance of certain prelates in the face of tyranny. There were the martyrs during the early centuries, Basil and

Ambrose, Pope Martin, Pius VII, the bishops in concentration camps under the Nazis, and so on. In connection with men like these one hears such comments as, "in those days there really were bishops", which betray both our disappointment with the normal state of affairs and our unspoken belief in the evangelical vocation of the episcopate. Consider, too, those conciliar assemblies of the tenth century which proclaimed the "peace of God" in an extraordinary atmosphere of enthusiasm and rejoicing.[1] More frequently, however, the hierarchy has contributed only indirectly to the development or the discernment of spiritual phenomena. (Examples can be found in the history of the foundation of religious orders or of the missionary enterprise.) In short, the institution, in virtue of its origin as of its history, appears to be polarized by the very spiritual activity which is its justification and its concern. It can also, of course, exist completely turned in on itself, intent on self-preservation and its "carnal" well-being. Torn between the vocation that comes to it "from above" and the pull of its existence in society, the Church's history is one of drama and tension. Many people cannot really look at it and see it as it is: thus the uncompromising apologists (who only recognize the spiritual power in the Church) and the systematic protesters (who have given up the idea of looking on the institution as a place for reception of the Spirit).

The ecclesial institution is fully expressed by the spiritual movement, while, on the other hand, the spiritual movement bears witness itself to a tendency to become institutionalized. A spiritual experience took place, perhaps, in a rare and blessed moment of encounter, a kairos in which case there is no need to point to anything more than a share in the quasi-immediacy. But the movement is not confined to the spiritual experience, even if it gives it meaning. It is a social fact which, if it is to emerge and become recognized, needs continuity coherence, instruments of communication, outward manifestations of allegiance, and celebrations—and any one of these can so quickly become institu-

---

[1] The charismatic character of these assemblies becomes clear when one reads, for example, the chronicler Raoul Glaber, who described the one at Le Puy-en-Velay in 990. Extracts from his text and those of contemporary writers will be found in Latreille, Delaruelle and Palanque, *Histoire du catholicisme en France* I (Paris, 1957), p. 236.

tionalized. The dream of "religionless Christianity" has been entertained more than once in the course of history, and has been a means of support for a few isolated individuals, but it will take its place only with difficulty in history and society—unless it is to betray itself and assume the characteristics of a "counter-church". Moreover, the concrete problem for the majority of spiritual movements was not whether to accept or reject all aspects of institution, but how to behave with regard to the ecclesial institution from which they had emerged. Should they support it, reform it, set themselves apart or create a new community (Church or State)? Whichever solution they chose, it always remained apparent that the institutional organization had a measure of importance as a framework and outward sign of the spiritual insight they wished to pass on.

To clarify the relationship between institutions and spiritual movements, one also needs to consider the Spirit's characteristic modes of action, a somewhat ambitious undertaking, but Scripture has a certain amount to say about it. Creative, loving liberty, the Spirit also is fidelity—fidelity to the word of Jesus for St John, to the message of the cross for St Paul (cf. 1 Cor. 2). This fidelity of the Spirit to the gospel as living force is extended to the promises of Christ in the institution (cf. Jn. 20. 22–23). These promises, it must be stressed, do not envisage any total and constant spiritualization of the ecclesial body, but rather the assistance of the Paraclete in those acts by which the Church, according to its particular calling, serves and reveals the Good News—preaching the word, the ministry of reconciliation, the Eucharist. To ignore the connection between the Spirit and these acts, accomplished with genuine faith, would be to make of the Spirit an impulsive and unreliable being. In our own day, the prayers of *epiclesis*, which in the majority of churches precede the celebration of the sacraments, well express both the fidelity expected of the Spirit where the gifts of God are concerned, and the impotence of the human acts and ritual elements to produce, of themselves, the spiritual action. By these prayers, the institution acknowledges its own relative nature and affirms all the more emphatically the power of the Spirit. On the other hand, if the action of the Spirit is revealed in the life of a Christian community, he cannot appear under the sign of fidelity alone, but rather in the fullness of what he is, creative, encouraging spontaneity, opposing all that smacks of the pseudo-spiritual. The theme of the presence of the Spirit in the churches should not be exploited in favour of a conservative interpretation or an appeal to passive obedience. The gift of this presence is not made in order that the community should find in it security and satisfaction but in order that it should go out of itself. In other words, if the Spirit is *already present* to the churches, it is to remind them that they are *not yet* spiritual.

It is precisely because ecclesial institutions, although pledged to the Spirit, are not yet spiritual, that movements grow up in their midst whose concern is to "hasten the time". More or less, according to circumstances, these movements are aware of what they have received from the Church, or else of what it lacks, hence the complexity of the relationship between them and the institution. History offers numerous examples of this complexity. One of the most interesting comes from the late twelfth and early thirteenth centuries. This period was particularly prolific in spiritual movements, and in less than a century one can watch them as, by turns, they oppose or support, step outside the limits or heal the breaches of the traditional Church—which is surely to exhaust the possible types of relationship between the "spiritual" and the institution.

II. In the History of the Twelfth Century Four Types of Relationship between Spiritual Movements and Institutions are Discernible

The twelfth century witnessed a kind of expansion in Western Europe—a demographic development and a renaissance of urban life, commerce and the distribution of money, literature and the arts. The crumbling feudal powers did not disappear, but were attacked from above and below, by the centralization of the French and English monarchies and by the "franchises" granted to cities. In a world less settled than that of the rural society of the later Middle Ages, not all were able to adapt to a less clearly defined way of life and to the growing power of money.

The Church had just made a supreme effort to free itself from the gilded chains with which it had allowed feudalism to bind it—this was the Gregorian reform which, from the second half of the eleventh century, worked towards an improvement in the recruitment and morals of the clergy. It provoked the first struggle between Church and State which is traditionally associated with two personalities (Gregory VII and Henry IV) and the Concordat of Worms which brought it to an end in 1122 assured the triumph of the Church. The lay-lords had to relinquish their privilege of investing "by the cross and the ring" the prelates in their vassalage. Now, in order to ensure the acceptance of this solution the papacy had wrought for itself a temporal power until then unparalleled, forced kings and emperors to stand down, extended its sovereignty to the Norman states in Italy, Tuscany, Spain, Hungary and the Holy Land, led the crusade, and so on. A paradoxical situation—establish it as one's goal to purify the institution and extricate it from compromising political entanglements, and to end up by assuring it an even more powerful position in this world.

This ecclesiastical domination was contested at the time, and the twelfth century is punctuated by struggles against the power of the Church. The conflict with the Empire was renewed under Frederick Barbarossa (1152–1190). The new political forces had no intention of allowing themselves to be hemmed in by the ecclesiastical authorities: the monarchy challenged the hierarchy (cf. the murder of Thomas à Becket, Archbishop of Canterbury in 1170); the city states rose up against prelates who upheld the feudal system; in Rome itself the republic (a reminder of antiquity) was proclaimed against the express will of the popes (between 1144 and 1155).

These struggles were spectacular but finally, by the close of the century, the "papal theocracy" and the power of the clergy had grown stronger. More serious, in one sense, for the Church, was the fact that it had disappointed a considerable section of the Christian people in their aspirations to "poverty" and purity of life. It had seemed, at one stage, that it encouraged these aspirations; when the official reformers of the eleventh century were struggling against corrupt priests and the feudal lords who supported them, they met with co-operation from popular and fairly turbulent lay movements, such as the "pataria" in Milan (between 1050 and 1075). One might have thought that renewal of the Church would take the form of promotion of the rights of ordinary people and the poor. The reality did not match up to their expectation; it should be no cause for surprise, therefore, that popular movements emerged once again in the twelfth century, protesting this time, however, not against simoniac priests, but against the entire institution, in the name of evangelical poverty.[2]

1. Radical Opposition to the Institution in Popular Movements at the Beginning of the Thirteenth Century

The ecclesiastical writers, St Bernard and Peter the Venerable, were upset by the virulence of the anti-clerical reactions provoked in their time by more or less enlightened preachers who enjoyed a popular following. They had before their eyes the example of Pierre de Bruis and his disciple Henri. Towards 1130, in Provence and then in Languedoc, these agitators burned crosses, lambasted priests (not just verbally either), forcing them to marry, and defied all authority. During the first decades of the century, Tanchelm (or Tanchelin) of Antwerp and the Breton Eude (or Eon) de l'Etoile had gone before them on this path of insurrection against the "established" Church.[3] Others were to follow, like Arnold of Brescia, who associated himself with the rebellion of the Romans against the temporal power of the popes, and Speroni. Although these men came to a bad end, executed by the authorities or by the crowd (as in the case of Pierre de Bruis at Saint Gilles-du-Gard, c. 1140), they had been able, over the years, to spread their message and gather disciples.

The movements swept along by these men were vehicles for an emotional protest rather than a doctrine. People have tried in vain to link them with Manichaean tendencies or with the

[2] We will be excused for simplifying the complicated question of the origins of the "heretico-popular" movements of the Middle Ages. Disappointment with the way the Gregorian reform turned out by no means explains everything. That it was an important factor appears from the way the word "patare" changed its meaning between the eleventh and twelfth centuries (it came to mean "heretic").

[3] These, too, had eleventh-century predecessors, but there is no evidence to suggest that they founded movements on the same scale as those we observe in the twelfth century.

Catharist heresy.[4] There is no evidence to be found in them of metaphysical speculation or of attempts to find a way of separating spirit from matter. They announced that the "judgment of God" was imminent—the Kingdom of the "Holy Ones" and the return of Christ. Above all they disputed every ecclesiastical appointment, and particularly significant in this connection are the teachings of the Petrobrusians (followers of Pierre de Bruis), treated as being of importance by Peter the Venerable in the treatise he wrote against them. They rejected infant baptism, which makes "the faith of the Church" mean something else besides the conviction of each individual believer; they called for the destruction of religious buildings and altars, and for the banning of singing from worship; they suppressed suffrages for the faithful departed, not out of want of respect for the dead, but quite obviously to deprive the clergy of their hold over the people. Their denial of the real presence in the Eucharist seemed, to St Bernard, to have been inspired by Berenger of Tours, but in spite of its virulence it was of no great theological significance and was a far cry from the subtleties of the schools: Pierre de Bruis merely denied that the body of Christ has remained at the disposal of an apostolic community since the resurrection.[5] Briefly, then, the message of the Petrobrusians can be summed up as an attack on all church property and against the temporal power of the clergy, the result, perhaps, of an urge to share the lot of the only "holy ones", the poor, without compromising in any way with the institutions of this world.

These protesters, in setting themselves up against the visible Church, also denounced society. Recent historians have been interested in the undeniable political implications of their movements. Too simplistic an interpretation must, however, be rejected—one which would make of the phenomenon a mere

---

[4] The Catholic authors of the eleventh and twelfth centuries have often contributed to the confusion of recent historians by calling all kinds of heretics "Manichaeans" on the basis of superficial similarities. On this point see R. Morghen, "Movimenti religiosi popolari nel periodo della riforma della Chiesa" in *Relazioni del X congresso intero di scienze storiche* III (Florence, 1955), pp. 333–56.

[5] See Peter the Venerable, *Contra Petrobrusianos* (Fearns' "Corpus Christianorum"), pp. 87, 150, 8–11.

episode in the class struggle. But we have no evidence that the campaigns of these preachers enjoyed success in any very clearly defined milieux. Their movements did not attract only, or even principally, the migrant workers (*vagi*) of the countryside; even less did they represent the aspirations of the ascendant middle class which was, however, still despised by the feudal nobility and neglected by the Church. Rather, knights and many clerics met together in them, with people from the lower classes.[6] It was not so much one class that found expression here as an entire society, which was thus able to develop its critical sense and learn to its own instability. From this point of view the obvious anarchy which we encounter in Tanchelm or Pierre de Bruis speaks simultaneously of the impossibility of living in the over-restrictive framework of feudalism and in fear of new forms of social organization. More specifically, these movements reacted against wealth and its power.

Perhaps one will be less ready to admit the spiritual import of these movements than their political significance. At first one is struck by the *naïveté*, the passion, the violence and occasionally the paranoia of the protagonists of religious insurrection (Tanchelm and Eon proclaimed themselves "sons of God"). Even genuine saints saw no more in Pierre de Bruis, Henri, or Arnold of Brescia than vulgar agitators or criminals. How can we rehabilitate them by carrying out in their favour a process of discernment of spirits that we would be unable to carry out for one of our contemporaries? And yet, if we must give up the idea of passing judgment on the spiritual quality of this or that personality, we can recognize in the upheaval they have created the echo of aspirations which are authentically spiritual and indicate the presence of the profoundest elements of Christianity.

In the first place, at the root of this popular excitement, there is a longing to return to the gospel. Peter the Venerable, an otherwise unsympathetic witness, vouches for this by the number

---

[6] Of the leaders of the movements, Eon was a knight, Henri a monk, Arnold a canon, and, later, Peter Valdes a rich merchant. In the twelfth century, as so often, there were many people who protested against their own class. See *Hérésies et sociétés dans l'Europe pre-industrielle, Communications et Débats du Colloque de Royaumont présentés par Le Goff* (Monton, 1968).

of scriptural quotations which he mentions in his refutations. He is well aware that "heretics" of this kind can only be got at by weapons of this kind.

The gospel, here, is the gospel read without glosses; direct contact with it was what they wanted, whence their marked distrust of the scholar who seeks to impose his own learning along with the message of the book. The leaders of the new movements voluntarily styled themselves illiterate (*sine litteris*), and if they were in any way educated, they disguised the fact. Apart from mistrust of the power of knowledge, this determination to ignore tradition was no doubt aimed at abolishing the centuries that separate us from the gospel, centuries which have erected the institution between the event and ourselves. Of all the Scriptures, Pierre de Bruis retained only the four gospels—no doubt in order to eliminate the history, that is to say the progressive and social character, of Christianity. This is an exaggerated version of the desire of every "spiritual": that the gospel should be immediately open and accessible to him.

For the protesters in question, the gospel is not only a book; it is a force which must turn our lives and our world upside-down. The characteristic signs of this force, from which the new age is to spring up, will be, not the permanence of the sacrament in the institution, but the occurrence of the unexpected, the reign of the poor, the overthrow of the powerful, joy in the midst of persecution. It was precisely these signs which the popular followers of Tanchelm or Pierre de Bruis looked for and wished, not, it is true, without a number of mistakes and misinterpretations, to give to the world. This is why their enthusiasm, without having actually to be canonized, does not seem entirely unrelated to the general spiritual quest.[7]

2. *Spiritual Movements as Supports for the Institution*

The Church answered the attacks of the anti-clericals with repression, with all the weight of its incarnational reality, with its social and cultural prestige, but also with its spiritual

[7] On this subject, in addition to works cited in previous notes, see Grundmann, *Religiöse Bewegungen im Mittelalter* (Hildesheim, 1961); Werner, *Pauperes Christi* (Leipzig, 1956); Borst, *Die Katharer* (Stuttgart, 1953), ch. 1.

vitality. New monastic orders were founded, more closely attached to the institution than was primitive monachism, orders of monk-clerks, prepared if need be, to leave the "leisure of contemplation" for a bishopric or a legation. Cîteaux, founded in 1098, is the model for this. The reform of the canons, which regained respect for the common life, for the sharing of goods and for the rule of St Augustine as practised by clerks of cathedrals, colleges and hospitals, went forward to the lasting benefit of the institution, and historians of the twelfth century have said a great deal about it. They have tended, however, to overlook the flowering of communities formed by lay people with the idea of putting the gospel message to practical effect. Fortunately, recent studies have thrown more light on the phenomenon. In the region of Vicenza, for example, small farmers went in for sharing their lands, their work and their life of prayer; these were married people, settled on their lands by the canons of the diocese, and their relations with the clergy were friendly, but they preserved the autonomy of their group. They belonged, no doubt, to that much more far-reaching trend, the "lay penitents", from whose midst Francis of Assisi would emerge.[8]

The originality and variety of these new forms of community life argue in favour of the spiritual vitality of a Church which was otherwise too administrative and bound to the political order. Evidently one would not expect to find among these orthodox groups the violent protest and the anarchy which are characteristic of "heretical" spirituals. However, the main lines of research, for the one as for the other, overlap more than one would have imagined at first. Practical living of the gospel, a thirst for return "to the life-style of the primitive Church", served as the principle for new reforms in the institution. Their literal interpretation of the Bible is sometimes naïve but always sincere. Cîteaux, created originally by pioneer monks, was virtually established in a desert among "savage beasts", so that they could escape from wealthy benefactors (cf. the *Exodium* of Stephen Harding). As the cen-

---

[8] See Meerseman and Adda, "Penitents ruraux au XIIe siécle" in RHE XLIX (1954), pp. 343–90; Mandonnet-Vicaire, "Les origines de l'ordo de poenitentia" in *Saint Dominique* II (Paris, 1937), pp. 295–308; M. D. Chenu, "Moines, clercs et laïcs au carrefour de la vie évangélique in RHE XLIX, pp. 74 ff.

tury went on it is true that the Cistercian Order became richer, but the practice of voluntary self-deprivation went side by side with preaching and the "care of souls" among the canons regular, especially the Premonstratensians (in the life of their founder, St Norbert, we read the saying usually applied to St Francis: "Naked, he followed the naked Christ").

Still on the subject of poverty, it was not so much the practice of asceticism which interested the "spiritual" of the twelfth century, as the joy of discovering the gospel in a living experience. Their desire for a fresh contact with the Christian sources comes out in their piety, and in this connection the works of St Bernard and other Cistercian masters (William of St Thierry and Aelred of Rievaulx) should be mentioned, along with those of the canons, Hugh and Richard of St Victor, and so on. Today we are struck by the affective quality of their devotion, their "psychological awareness". With them we are as far removed from learned, objective speculation as we are from the practices of popular religion in the late Middle Ages with their excessive tendency to materialize. The new spirituality was based on desire for a heartfelt and openly expressed relationship with the realities of faith. Thus Bernard is someone who speaks out of his own experience to those who want to experience in their turn the tenderness or the sufferings of Jesus in his humanity, the friendship of the Virgin, or the coming of the Word into the soul, and who wish to learn, above all, how one comes to love God. His mysticism is clearly dependent on that desire for immediacy and openness which is characteristic of the spiritual movement.

The charm of St Bernard (1090–1153), of whom William of St Thierry said that people who were prejudiced against him began to love him as soon as they saw him, was that of an eminently charismatic personality. In him we see that inspiration and submission to the institution can go together. A conservative prophet, you might say. Conservative he was indeed—this feudal spirit who remained tied to feudal ideas even for the mode of government and expansion of his abbey at Clairvaux, who defended popes and their temporal power, and who was the driving force behind the second crusade; this polemicist who took issue with the bolder theologians of his century, Gilbert de la Porrée and Abélard—poor uncomprehending Bernard! But how could he, who was able to savour the spiritual mysteries directly, be expected to understand anything of the methodological doubt of the dialectician? To an even greater extent, however, he was charismatic—this defender of the "Church militant" who put his contemporaries to shame for their anti-semitic pogroms; this friend of monks, so easy-going and humorous in the right place (think of his description of the gargoyles at Cluny); this man who advised prelates with unparalleled frankness and who brought peace to cities; this tender reassuring ascetic. One can imagine that Luther enjoyed the treatise *On Consideration* dedicated to Eugene III, one-time novice of St Bernard. In it the pope is invited not to imitate his venerable predecessors by wasting his time, to humble himself, and to look on his flatterers as his worst enemies.

3. *A Spiritual Force the Institution could not understand*

The "poor of Lyons" or Waldensians emerged initially as a kind of "lay penitents'" movement, in search of poverty and the right to preach freely. Their founder, a rich merchant of Lyons, Peter Waldo, moved by the song of a minstrel, sold his goods, left home, set about translating the Scriptures and adopted the way of life of the wandering preacher (in 1173 or a little later). Men and women gathered round him and followed his example. Their aim was not to attack the institutional Church, but to provide it with the example of a community free of secular attachments and acknowledging no leader but Christ, of an unsophisticated and provocative approach to the gospel. They set out to combat heretics, such as the Cathari, with no other arms but word and example.[9] !

Good relations between the Waldensians and the institution did not last, in spite of Peter Waldo's efforts to get himself accepted by the archbishop of Lyons and Pope Alexander III. In 1183 the sect was excommunicated, driven out of Lyons and, in the following year, formally condemned by Pope Lucius III. Perhaps it had caused scandal by the violence of its invective against the

[9] See Gonnet, *Il Valdismo mediaevale* (Torre-Pellice, 1942); Solge, *Die ersten Waldenser* (Berlin, 1967); Dondaine, *Aux origines du Valdéisme* (Archivum Fr. Praed., 1949); Thonzelier, *Catharisme et Valdéisme* (Paris, 1966); *Cahiers de Fanjeaux* 2 (Toulouse, 1967).

rich and against the corrupt members of the clergy (not unusual at the time); or else by the role it accorded to women in the work of preaching? But the immediate cause of their condemnation was their arrogation to themselves of the freedom to preach, if need be without permission from the clergy.

Was this just the result of misunderstanding on the part of some minor official? Less, certainly, than one might think. The institution tends to react against free-lance preachers, who want to make the gospel more alive and relevant, because it fears their incompetence—and also because their appearance in competition with bishops and priests implies a denunciation of the insufficiencies and spiritual torpor of the latter. The comments of an English cleric, who saw the first Waldensians in Rome in 1179, undoubtedly reflect the feelings of frustration generated by these "paupers" who made use of their poverty in order to usurp the functions of another "order".

Peter Waldo, for his part, could not bear not to preach. Considering himself to be invested with power from on high, he declared that "it is better to obey God than men", and however one may be inclined to judge his behaviour, one cannot but regret this failure to welcome the gifts of prophecy and preaching in the Church of the twelfth century. An over-exclusive and self-complacent confidence in the link between the Spirit and the established hierarchy is doubtless at the root of this want of openness.

4. *A Spiritual Movement integrated into the Institution*

Once they had been excommunicated, the Waldensians spread throughout Languedoc, the Rhinelands and Lombardy (where they joined forces with the "Humiliati" whose history then becomes linked with theirs). They lived by begging (or, in Italy, by weaving wool); they were not allowed to take oaths, at that time an important element in social life, and preached absolute nonviolence. They counted it a blessing to be persecuted by the Church, but did not reject the sacraments of "bad priests" (at the beginning at least); they created new rites for themselves, such as "the breaking of bread".

St Dominic and the anti-Albigensian preacher of the Catholic Church in Languedoc could not fail to notice the zeal of the Waldensians in the country round about, and their success with peoples who hungered for example rather than for words. They set out to bring them round to their own position, and in part they succeeded. A Waldensian group, headed by the writer Durand of Huesca, agreed to submit, under certain conditions, to the Church of Rome, and obtained permission to preach to popular audiences and to live "in the Waldensian manner", that is in poverty as itinerant mendicants (1209). These were the "poor Catholics". In 1201 another group of Waldensians in Italy, led by Bernard Prim, had likewise been reinstated in the Church of Rome.

Such reinstatements, carried out under the auspices of Pope Innocent III, constitute an extremely interesting compromise between the institution and the charismatic movements. The latter agreed to moderate their anti-clericalism and to allow themselves to be guided by authority in the carrying out of their work of preaching. The institution recognized the advantages of lay preaching (to be distinguished, it is true, from that other, "doctrinal" variety which was the sole preserve of clerics), and beyond this there lies the further recognition of the relative nature of its relationship with the One who bestows his charisms as seems best to him. In order to live in harmony with one another, men must learn how to recognize their mutual relativity.

III. CONCLUSION

In the debate between movements and institutions we tend instinctively to favour the "spiritual"; they stand for life, enthusiasm, and rejection of compromise, for the capacity to surprise, and for communion. The institution, on the other hand, is recognized as possessing wisdom, a clear and universal language, and the task of passing on rites and pedagogical images. This unequal distribution of merits does not of necessity lead to conflict, and can even give rise to an awareness of complementarity. History, as we have seen, offers examples of this. The question is, therefore—under what conditions can institution and movement achieve a climate of mutual acceptance and become integrated one with the other? Let us beware of cut-and-dried answers—general laws cannot be deduced from the past, but, at best, only a number of wise reflections. We therefore offer some of our own.

(a) In order to explain the resistance of the churches to spiritual trends, the sociological burden of the institution is invariably brought into the argument—its link with political powers, that is, or with economic forces, its fear lest its traditions or its hierarchical structure should be overthrown. This point of view, whose merits we recognize, has been put forward so often recently, that it would be tedious to dwell on it.

The institution, which so often rejects the "spiritual", has no wish, however, to despise or forget the Spirit. Anxious to affirm his presence in their midst, they quickly forget that "he blows where he wills"; docility to the Spirit becomes somehow identified and confused with the duty of obedience to their own injunctions. They overrate themselves as spiritual instruments. This explains their all too frequent mistrust of any who claim to speak prophetically, unless they themselves have authorized them to speak, or of any who set out to create new patterns of community, outside the ones they themselves have recognized. In the course of history, confrontations between the traditional Church and the charismatic movements have centred, in the main, on the right to preach freely and the forms to be taken by evangelical poverty, and only secondarily on the principles of political ethics from which the "spiritual" claimed to draw their inspiration. The mystics, who, to achieve union with God, seemed to bypass ecclesiastical intermediaries, were feared almost as much as the charismatic revolutionaries, and in this rejection of a spiritual element which would have been foreign to it, it is easy to recognize a sociological reflex of the ecclesial body, an instinct for self-preservation (the protection of society at large, in spite of what some may think, seems to me to play a subordinate role).

This instinct for self-preservation can be controlled, and the churches throughout the ages have controlled it more or less effectively, which explains their varying degrees of openness to spiritual movements. Innocent III, for example, departing from the practice of his predecessors, allowed first the "poor Catholics" and then St Francis to remain within the institution while they denounced its lack of spirituality. He was hoping for an abundant outpouring of the Spirit on a Church which recognized the relative nature of its spiritual wealth, and pointed out that the community of believers lives in a state of tension between the structures which await the Spirit, and the actual arrival of the One who is to come.

(b) The charismatic movements were not always concerned to become integrated into the institution. Some, however, judged it good to preserve their bond with it. They hoped for a more complete manifestation of the power of the gospel, but did not look on their belonging to the Church as being something prejudicial to this. Thus charismatics expect to hear the Word of God in the immediacy of the present moment; but others are aware that this Word is also a memory preserved by an institution rich in experience—and a memory which both complements and relativizes the discovery of the present moment. The prophet can afford to let himself be guided by the guardians of tradition, since he believes there is continuity between the Spirit of Jesus and the Jesus of the apostolic community.

In addition, the "spiritual" often succumb to the temptation of taking a sign of the Spirit for the Spirit himself; they make an absolute of their charism rather in the same way that the institution makes an absolute of its dogmas and its hierarchy, and so it is essential for their spiritual welfare that some control be exercised over them, or that they should be required to account for themselves, in the spirit of the gospel; more often than not, it is the churches who are expected to carry out this task, this service, and this is a delicate point, because on the one hand, not all the "spiritual" are willing to be called to account in this way, and on the other the churches do not always know how to create the climate of trust which is indispensable if their judgment is to be accepted.

The "spiritual" are faced, also, with the threat of "élitism" or even of sectarianism: they sometimes succeed in alienating the masses by their esotericism or their demands and then justify what has happened only too glibly. The churches have, in general, a greater concern for the multitude. They are sometimes accused, and not always mistakenly, of demagogy, but this concern of theirs for universality and for adaptation to the needs of all is also the reflection of a characteristically evangelical preoccupation. It is often in order not to cut themselves off from the main body of Christians under the pretext that they are called to higher things, that the "spiritual" have, in the past, adopted a patient and tolerant attitude towards the Church—for how can one separate oneself lightheartedly from these crowds who are the object of the Lord's compassion? It may be that a certain degree of mediocrity must inevitably exist in the churches as the pendant of that compassion for the multitude which is part of their heritage. Even so, the churches must not betray the multitudes for whom they claim to have responsibility. More than one celebrated protest against the institution has risen out of the conviction that a people was being betrayed by the ecclesiastical hierarchy: one can think of John Hus or of Savonarola, and who would condemn men like this today? And how is one to recognize the evangelical origin of responsibility for the multitude when that responsibility is exercised in the least evangelical of ways?

Reconciliation is not always possible, but one is glad to recall, in closing, those spiritual movements which, while they jealously guarded their liberty, learnt how to live within a Church that is naturally weighed down by its incarnational presence in society. Prophetic inspiration *can* unite harmoniously with the traditional faith, and new ways of living in the Spirit with concern not to allow "one of these little ones to perish", for whom Christ came.

Translated by Sarah Fawcett

Fernando Urbina

Movements of Religious Awakening and the Christian Discernment of Spirits

AROUND 1968 the Western world saw the beginning of what has become a progressive growth of spiritual movements, the fact as usual antedating the reflection it provokes. But as these movements become more intense, and affect ever-widening groups of people, especially young people, the Church is beginning to inquire into what their significance might be.

Finding an explanation for a fact involves first finding a word with which to describe it. The churches have their memories of similar movements of "religious awakening" in the past, and it is as this that they are beginning to be known in some quarters. The word "awakening" has the advantage of having no precise, technical meaning in traditional spiritual terminology, so the compound "religious awakening" is sufficiently wide in its application to take in a wide variety of such phenomena.

These waves of religious and spiritual renovation have posed many problems for the Church, upsetting institutional equilibrium and received modes of thought. Throughout history it has been necessary to inquire into their meaning so as to decide on a suitable spiritual and pastoral approach to dealing with them. Traditionally, certain criteria "for the discernment of spirits" have been called upon to answer these questions and anxieties.

What these criteria are and their value for our day need examining, and I propose to do this by taking some of the "Christian criteria for the discretion of spirits" witnessed by the tradition of the faith and attempting to apply them to the particular problems posed by the new "movements of religious awakening".

I. Some Traditional Criteria for the Discernment of Spirits

"Discernment of spirits" is a traditional phrase in the vocabulary of faith, being found in the New Testament (1 Cor. 12. 10), and has a practical and precise meaning when applied to the questions we are asking. It means the capacity of judging the value to faith of spiritual movements that arise in the individual or collective consciousness and of thereby forming the vital practice of the believer and of the community.

Reference to a specific spiritual tradition will take us deeper into the meaning of the phrase, and I propose to concentrate on that of a particular moment in the history of the spirituality of the Western churches: baroque Catholic spirituality, as epitomized in two witnesses of exceptional significance on this point, St Ignatius of Loyola and St John of the Cross. Both have their roots in an earlier situation, that of the "movements of religious awakening" of the early sixteenth century, an historical background of intense spirituality shared by the other Western traditions that came into being at that time—Lutherans, Reformed Churches, various evangelical, spiritualist and illuminist movements, etc.[1] Following that, I shall examine the "spiritual criteria" of the tradition common to all the Christian churches, as evidenced in the New Testament.

1. The Spiritual Criteriology of St Ignatius

Rahner has demonstrated the value of a "theological re-reading" of the *Spiritual Exercises* that goes beyond a formal, schematic approach and opens the way to its deeper meaning.[2]

(a) *The Criterion of the Spirit.* The "choices"[3] are the heart of the *Spiritual Exercises*, detailing the process of radical decision involved in conversion. For St Ignatius the most valuable part of the process is not the "third time of choice" (which consists in

---

[1] L. Febvre, *Au cœur religieux du XVIme siècle* (Paris, 1957); M. Bataillon, *Erasme et l'Espagne* (Paris, 1937).

[2] K. Rahner, *Dynamism in the Church* (Quaest. Disp. 5, London and New York), p. 196.

[3] *Obras Completas de San Ignacio de Loyola* (Bib. de autores crist., Madrid, 1952), p. 194.

a rational analysis based on general principles and norms), but the first and second times, consisting of a form of openness to the Spirit that cannot be deduced from general principles of previous situations and so can take on new forms in each age.

This dimension of "openness to the Spirit" in Ignatian criteriology has a bearing on our present historical situation. Spiritual and pastoral practice has to be open to the action of the Spirit with its radical novelty, which is a sign of the eschatological *novum*.

(b) *The Criterion of the Gospel.* In the *Exercises*, the "imperative" of the Spirit refers to the "evangelical principles". If the believing conscience, open to the infinity of the Spirit, makes the right choice according to the will of God (Rom. 12. 2), this is because the spirit of Jesus has taken shape in it through its meditation on and contemplation of the deeds and sayings of the master.

In the "meditation on two standards", Ignatius provides one of the evangelical keys to the "discernment of spirits": the temptations in the desert, which show the fundamental contradiction between the two spirits, that of Jesus and that of the "prince of this world". But the Church of the baroque age failed to observe this discernment in its institutional and pastoral practice, its powerful triumphalism and identification with the ruling power being more in line with the "power and the glory" of this world (Lk. 4. 6) than with the spirit of the gospel.

(c) *Action and Contemplation.* The "calling of the temporal king", stripped of its baroque imagery, gives us another evangelical key: Jesus' calling of his disciples (Mk. 1. 16), which is a call not to an escapist mysticism, but to a prophetic involvement. In the Ignatian tradition, *"contemplativi in actione"* indicates not only a temporal rhythm ("a time for action and a time for contemplation"), but a transcendental dialectic: "human action" becomes "a gift of God".

2. *The Spiritual Criteriology of St John of the Cross*

St John of the Cross takes on a particular significance as a witness to the Western Christian tradition today, owing to the interest taken by "movements of religious awakening" in mystical experience and contemplative activity. The great Spanish mystic also has a particular significance for the ecumenical dialogue of spiritualities: at least in some elements of his experience and language, which need a more detailed analysis to be understood fully, he shows a close affinity to Eastern mysticism, but his radical theology of faith finds its closest affinity, which has not yet been studied, within the field of Christian spirituality, to the original Lutheran experience.

St John of the Cross displays a fascinating mystery, which has not yet been fully deciphered and which makes him doubly interesting for the modern mind: the enigma of his texts, of his language and of the historical origins of his contemplative tradition. The texts, at least the major ones which have not survived in manuscript form, are only known to us in deeply mutilated versions. It was only in 1912, thanks to the work of Fr Gerardo de S. Juan de la Cruz, that it was possible to begin to read them with some completeness,[4] and there are still some major textual problems unresolved. Neither can the full meaning of his writings in all their linguistic density be fully extracted until we can uncover the inner process of their gestation and resolve another enigma, the historical origin of his sources.

These remain veiled in silence. We do not know what connection St John of the Cross had with the Spanish and European "movements of religious awakening" of the first half of the sixteenth century and the earlier currents of mysticism.[5] Any explicit dependence on sources is veiled in the lack of contemporary references, and the written language has become more opaque in the process of elaboration, grown drier and more impoverished as it moves from the original freshness of the poetry, through the drafting of the oldest texts, to the excessively overloaded conceptual and scholastic style of the latest state of the

[4] G. de S. Juan de la Cruz, *Edición crítica de las obras de San Juan de la Cruz* (Toledo, 1912). Most recent bibliography in, L. del SS. Sacramento, *Vida y Obras de San Juan de la Cruz* (Madrid, 1972), pp. 985–1011.

[5] J. Baruzi, *St Jean de la Croix et le problème de l'expérience mystique* (Paris, 1924); Dom Ph. Chevallier, *Le cantique spirituel de St Jean de la Croix* (Paris, 1930); P. Silverio de Sta Teresa, *Obras de San Juan de la Cruz, doctor de la Iglesia* (Burgos, 1929); J. Orcibal, *St Jean de la Croix et les mystiques rhéno-flamands* (Bruges, 1966); E. de la Virgen del Carmen, *San Juan de la Cruz y sus escritos* (Madrid, 1969).

text. There is a reason for this: the repression exercised in Spain by the Inquisition at the time.

Having adverted to the objective difficulties standing in the way of a deep and authentic reading of the texts, let us nevertheless try to distinguish some of his basic spiritual criteria which might be valid for our age.

(a) *Fantasy and Reality.* One of the characteristics of the spiritual movements that sprang up in the West around 1968 as a protest against a suffocatingly utilitarian, technocratic and positivist cultural climate was the rediscovery of the value of imagination and desire, and of the poetic and symbolic language in which to express them. St John of the Cross crystallizes a dialectic of the imagination in his great symbols: the "going out", the "night", the "mountain", the "nuptials" and the "flame of love". He also expresses a dynamic of desire that has not yet been adequately explored, but which forms the deepest strand of meaning in the poems, and loses its linguistic force in the prose commentaries, especially in the second draft of the *Canticle*, which is overloaded with scholastic distinctions.

But his expressions of imagination and desire, without losing the basic radicalism of the strength of his quest, are filtered through an inner discipline that transcends the arbitrariness of instinct, any frivolity of feeling and any escape from the realities of life. His "going out" is not a going out from reality, but a discovery of its ultimate significance, which does not deny the solidity of material things, but rather sees through it to the heart of reality: absolute love.

(b) *Sobriety and Splendour.* Some varieties of the current "movements of religious awakening", particularly the Pentecostalist ones, are enthusiastic in their manner of expression, while others follow a line of more sober contemplation. Without denying the possible values of the first variety—total expression of the body, the "joy of the feast", reaction against a repressive culture excessively orientated to technical work, etc.—one has to recognize that the contemplative serenity of the second is more in line with the spiritual criteria of St John of the Cross.

His texts unfold the dialectic of a "sobriety that hides a splendour": the symbols of the *Canticle* and the *Flame of Living Love* point to a real experience (they are not metaphors, which express an idea, but symbols, which express an experience). But they are clothed in expressions of sobriety in social behaviour, moderation of style and a denial of the need for "immediacy" felt by the small enthusiastic community, impatient of the time-scale proper to the "time of faith".

(c) *"Mystic time" and "Time of Faith"*. The experience described by the contemplative of Ávila requires a slow rhythm, unfolding in a long process of "lights and shades", "absences" and "presences", whose symbolic keys are the going out and the night, which signify basic movements of the time of faith. The contemplative elements in St John of the Cross, though formulated in the Dionysian tradition of passivity, are referred essentially to an experience of faith bathed in the light of the word of God. So his essential "spiritual criterion" is the assimilation of the mystical tradition to the prophetic tradition.

(d) *Celebration of the Gratuitous*. The Uruguayan theologian Juan Luis Segundo has described the new "theology of the death of God" of 1963–70 as a fruit of the closed system of Western capitalism,[6] which reduces man to the status of a cog in a machine and leaves no room for opening on to the transcendent. In the utilitarian and repressive world of technocrats and police forces, there is no room for either gratuitous celebration or prophetic criticism. Since 1968, a sector of the youth of the world has rediscovered prophetic criticism, the gratuitous act, the absolute value of joy, festive celebration and mystical contemplation, for which there is no place in the semantic mould of the System.

St John of the Cross's "Flame of living love" possesses this gratuitous character of pure celebration of the absolute joy of love as the intimate feast of the total Dialogue. This spiritual criterion of gratuitousness is what ordains the ultimate meaning of the practice of faith. It is the doxological tension of St Paul that Sr Isabel of the Trinity made the basic rationale of her life: "created for the praise of glory". In St John of the Cross this celebration is (still) intimate and secret. The mystical secret is

[6] Proceedings of the Assembly of Latin-American Theology on "Faith and Social Change in Latin America", held at the Escorial from 8–15 Aug. 1972.

linked to the sexual secret; the splendour of the total encounter between man and woman as an absolute incarnation of dialogue is a sacrament of the total encounter between man and God. Only in the parousia will hidden splendour and festive social celebration come together in the pure, transparent vision of glory. But this shining secret of contemplation and celebration can already be glimpsed in the night of faith, as a sign of eschatological hope.

3. The Criteriology of the New Testament

St Ignatius and St John of the Cross, as qualified witnesses of the Western tradition, refer us back to the basic witness of the whole Christian spiritual tradition, the New Testament.

(a) *A locus classicus: 1 Corinthians 12–14.* This is where we find the original expression of "discernment of spirits": *"Diakrisis Pneumaton"* (1 Cor. 12. 10). The isolation of this text from its overall context in the New Testament has led to a reductive interpretation of the discernment of spirits, as though this were a very specialized function of "spiritual fathers" engaged in the "direction of consciences" (or the resolution of the particular problem of deciding on priestly or religious vocations). Lost to sight was the fact that for St Paul "discernment" had a radical and overall function in Christian life: it is the very dynamic of a faith open to the spirit and not dependent on rules and regulations that bind it to a static past (2 Cor. 13. 5; 1 Cor. 11. 28; 1 Thess. 5. 19–22; Gal. 6. 4; Rom. 12. 3; Phil. 1. 9–10; Eph. 5. 8–10). This practice of faith makes it possible, as we have seen in the "choices" of St Ignatius, to grasp the newness of the age in fidelity to the gospel.

(b) *Pauline Sobriety and its Basis: the Time of the Cross.* Paul has no strong reproof for enthusiastic spirits—he himself has experienced the gift of tongues and ecstasy. But in his first letter to the Corinthians he gives a counsel of spiritual serenity and Christian realism.

The enthusiasm of the community at Corinth can be seen as a result of the special situation of people who saw themselves living in imminent expectation of the Second Coming. The closeness of the resurrection in the past and the coming in the future took the weight off the intermediate stage of history and the task of living in it. Christian experience became reduced to a pure "mysticism of evasion", not because the Corinthians (any more than the Thessalonians) were evading time, but simply because time no longer had any meaning, was about to come to an end.

Two thousand years later we can see that Paul was right when, faced with the exuberant enthusiasms of the Corinthians, he reminded them that they were living in the time of the Cross (1 Cor. 17. 31). He told the Romans that this time of faith was a time of hope and patience (Rom. 8. 25), in which we have to experience the "birth pangs of the world" (Rom. 8. 22).

(c) *Tongues and Spirits.* In 1 Cor. 12. 4 the principle of plurality in the community appears, related to a higher principle of unity: "There are varieties of gifts, but the same Spirit."

The New Testament contains an indication of the gospel's capacity to mould itself to a variety of tongues and spiritual traditions (a basic fact symbolized by the "divers tongues" of the apostles' preaching at Pentecost). Some years ago, Bultmann, tying earlier studies together, stressed the existence of mysterious and mystical strains in Pauline language: "it must be observed that there is a deep connection between Paul and Hellenic mysticism". But Bultmann immediately qualified this statement by pointing out the specific characteristics of the Pauline teaching on faith: mystical experience remains something subordinate and secondary to this basic line: "Paul certainly recognizes ecstasy, but for him it is merely a particular charism, not the specific Christian way of life".[7] C. H. Dodd, while recognizing the closeness of the language of St John (and of the New Testament in general) to certain traditions stemming from Platonism, Hermeticism, etc., likewise stresses the specific character of Christian spirituality: "In the New Testament, these Hellenistic influences are always secondary. The guiding norm is that determined by the original impulse of Christianity itself."[8] This is not simply a linguistic debate among specialists, but something much more

[7] R. Bultmann, *Das Problem der Ethik bei Paulus*, col. in *Exegetica* (Tübingen, 1967), pp. 49 and 59.
[8] C. H. Dodd, *The Bible and the Greeks* (London, 1964), pp. 247–8; *idem, The Fourth Gospel* (Cambridge, 1965), pp. 1–130.

fundamental that concerns Christian spiritual practice. The New Testament used the riches of other spiritual traditions, but subordinates them to the:

(d) *Original Unity of the Gospel.* The principle of the unity of the Spirit expressed in 1 Cor. 12. 4 refers to the objective (transcendental) unity of the gospel: the Spirit confesses Jesus (1 Cor. 12. 3). Is it possible to speak of an "evangelical spirituality"? The plurality of spiritual traditions contains certain types. In New Testament times there were basically two (this is oversimplifying somewhat, but I believe it to be valid in practice). Firstly, there are the *mystical traditions of salvation*—in the West, the "mystery cults", gnostic tendencies, hermetic currents, Platonism and neo-Platonism, Stoicism itself and in the East, the Buddhist traditions, classical Hinduism, etc., representing a type of spirituality that finds salvation in flight from the world and from history. Secondly, there are the *prophetic traditions,* that see salvation (a gift of God) in the midst of the historical compromise. Which type can the spirituality of Jesus be said to belong to?

I believe the answer to be clear. The message of salvation preached by Jesus is basically a prolongation (and for believing Christians a fulfilment) of the prophetic line. Jesus proclaims the imminence of the Kingdom announced by the prophets of Israel (**Mk.** 1. 15) and the realization of this announcement in the eschatological hour of his gospel (Lk. 4. 16–21).

(e) *Incorporation of Mystical Spirituality into Prophetic.* How can these two principles of "plurality" and "original unity of the gospel" be combined? We have already seen that the New-Testament contains elements of the mystical languages of Hellenism, and this presence of mysticism in the Christian spiritual tradition became more pronounced in the course of history, through St Augustine and Pseudo-Dionysius in the West, and penetrating the East also. St John of the Cross is an outstanding example of the fusion of the two religious traditions, prophetic and mystical, and of the subordination of this fusion to the central line of faith.

In the criterion of "Christian discernment of spirits" it is the "contemplative and ecstatic spirit" that is subordinated to the prophetic spirit, and not vice versa. The criterion of faith, taken from the gospel, took in the religious values of the contemplative experience, but purified them of their "evasive tendencies".

Mysticism, in the community of the Church, possesses an "auxiliary function of consolation". The contemplative possesses a social charism of being shot through with peace and serenity which enables him to console and inspire his brethren in the hard and necessary struggle of life. This is why his special experience will always be a particular charism, and secondary in relation to the central line of faith.

(f) *The Prophet as "Man of God" and "Man of the People"*. There is one reason that explains the ease with which contemplative spirituality has been "injected" into the prophetic tradition. Despite their formal differences, there is one horizon on which they converge: both refer to a "transcendent, divine, sacred experience", but in the prophet this experience, instead of remaining locked up in the intimacy of his being, impels him to proclaim it in society.

With this sacred reality inside him, the prophet is a "man of God", but this does not lead him to evasion, but rather to social involvement and so he is also a "man of the people".

We can see this in the great figures that the Christian spiritual tradition took later as its models: Moses is the man to whom "God speaks face to face as though to a friend" (Ex. 33. 11), but he is also the man who led his people out of slavery (Ex. 3. 7–10). Elijah listened to God on the mountain (1 Kings 9–13) but stood up to King Ahab over his injustice to the unfortunate Naboth (1 Kings 21. 1–23). Mary, after the supreme sacred experience of the Annunciation (Lk. 1. 26–38), did not take refuge in ecstasy, but went off to help a poor woman in need (Lk. 1. 39–45). Jesus did not hide himself in the monastery of Qumran, but involved himself in practical justice, truth and love, till he died at the hands of the powers of the world. A more careful look at the nature of Jesus' involvement will show us the "supreme criterion" of Christian spirituality.

(g) *The Criterion of the Incarnation*. This is the criterion of the "blood and water" of St John's Gospel, and of the "spirit that confesses Jesus Christ come in the flesh" of St John's first letter.

In the christological struggles of the third and fourth centuries this "criterion of salvation" received a classic formulation: "what is not taken on is not saved".

In his saving action, Christ effectively takes on the reality of history and his saving power reaches to the heart of the world and the people. The central act of salvation (the death of Christ) is a slice of life at its most basic, densest, most alienated and despised: the death of a slave. This fundamental meaning of the death of Christ has been traduced by Constantinian theology which made the symbol of the Cross a sceptre for the kings of this world. This betrayal then found support through the centuries on the part of ecclesiastical institutions that identified themselves with the powerful and the rich. Mysticism of evasion also dissimulates the real demands of the sort of justice and love put forward in the gospels. So the conscience of the rulers of the world—be they politicians, generals or ecclesiastics—is lulled into a sense of well-being.

Only if spiritual forces take on the hard reality of the world can the world be saved, because "what is not taken on is not saved". And this becomes doubly urgent as the body of the world swells to immense proportions and the forces of death are unleased: the oppression of man by man, the social life that covers this oppression, the violence that stems from it. . . .

(h) *Priestly Spirituality*. One characteristic of the new movements of religious awakening is their rediscovery of sacral values and the rites of worship. This is one of many signs of an opening in the closed horizon of secularism.

The spiritual tradition of Israel has a central axis which is "priestly worshipping, sacral", making Israel "a praying people" so that in its feasts and its life it can celebrate the glory of God. The historical relationship between this priestly tradition and the spirituality of the prophets has polarized the differences between them, but this should not obscure their basic unity of meaning. They can be seen converging to the point where this unity is fully achieved—according to the New Testament—in Jesus Christ.

The Christian spiritual tradition, based on the apostolic witness, maintains the primacy of the service of the glory of God, but, once again, this does not involve flight from the world or its tasks. Since Jesus, according to the Letter to the Hebrews, penetrated the Veil of the Holy of Holies (Heb. 9. 1–14; 10. 19–22), this has significantly remained torn (Mt. 27. 51) because access to God is now open to all and sacred space is now the whole universe, in which the Father is adored in "spirit and in truth" (Jn. 4. 23). So believers do not hide behind the walls of a stone temple to present their sacrifice to glory, but make of their bodies a living sacrifice (Rom. 12. 1). The glory of God, celebrated by the eschatological and eucharistic community, not only includes, but requires as an intrinsic moment in the process of its realization, the transformation of the world into the Kingdom of God, the Kingdom of justice, truth, peace and love among men (Is. 11. 1–9; 61. 1–3).

II. Applying the Criteria to Particular Cases

1. The new movement of religious awakening is encouraging dialogue between spiritual traditions of different branches of Christianity and different religions. This dialogue offers great possibilities for a new fullness of spirituality. It is a fruitful contribution of sacral and contemplative values in a world increasingly menaced by exteriorization, positivism, anguish and violence. It could mean a greater incorporation of the infinite and multiform richness of the Spirit at a time when we need an increase of spirit if we are to take on the vast growth of the body of the world.

2. We still need a "discernment of spirits" to enable us to distinguish the genuine from the false, from the point of view of faith, which is the point of view of the total salvation of man and of the whole world. We have already seen some of these criteria of discernment at work in our Christian tradition.

These criteria enable us to consider particular cases.

The countries where man's oppression by man is seen with particular intensity—the responsibility for it lies ultimately with the powers that be accumulated in the rich and powerful nations —show the debatable elements of some aspects of the post-1968 movements of religious awakening with particular force.

At a meeting of "secular missionaries" (a religious group of deep, Christ-centred spiritual life, but deeply involved in the real

problems of life) held in Madrid, it emerged that some of these
"new spiritual groups" had begun to appear in working-class
areas. But the boys and girls who came under the influence of
these movements appeared passive and indifferent to brutal social
realities, compared to others who were perhaps less religious but
more capable of involving themselves on the side of those who
were suffering from those realities. In Bolivia, a "preacher of
Jesus", from California, has appeared lately and assembled a considerable following of young people, but again the message is one
of pure spirituality and flight from the world.[9]

These are of course just particular examples that cannot pre-
tend to embrace the whole spectrum of the new movements of
religious awakening. But similar cases can be multiplied, and
must lead us to take a critical attitude to at least some aspects
of these movements, not on simple "political" grounds, but based
on strictly evangelical criteria of discernment.

3. In effect, the ultimate theological *locus* that determines the
radical meaning of the "discernment of spirits" (*"diakrisis pneumaton"*) is the *krisis*: the eschatological hour of God's judgment:
"krisis tou kosmou toutou" (Jn. 12. 31). The meaning and form
of this judgment can be seen in the parable of judgment (Mt.
25. 31–46): "I was hungry and you gave me food, I was thirsty
and you gave me drink, I was a stranger and you welcomed me,
I was naked and you clothed me, I was sick and you visited me,
I was in prison and you came to me . . . as you did it to one of the
least of these my brethren, you did it to me."

4. Finally, another real risk that has to be "discerned"—a risk
often visible in the new movements, particularly in circles of
young people, both in their spirituality and in their social involvement—is that of impatience for immediacy, which leads the
"spirituals" to an over-hasty quest for ecstasy (which is related
to the quest for paradise through the short-cut of hallucinatory
drugs), and the "committed" to the utopian pretensions of immediate total revolution. This is a temptation that seems to re-
produce the features of millenniarist impatience of earlier epochs.[10]

There is one objective reason that leads people to this sort of

---

[9] *La Prensa*, Lima, 24 Feb. 1973.
[10] N. Cohn, *The Pursuit of the Millennium* (London, 1970).

temptation. It is the suffocation of living in a dehumanizing social situation and the frustration of banging one's head against the wall of accumulated, repressive power and the social lie that drugs the people and so holds the wall up. It is a concrete barrier into which the best impulses of young people too often crash, burning themselves out in the process and ending up either in the ashes of compromise with bourgeois values or in the furnace of violent "radicalization", politically ineffective and destructive of the personality.

The presence of communities of faith and movements of religious awakening can actually be a help in preventing this risk of the best impulses being burnt out. With their celebrations, their sacraments and their contemplation, provided these are free from evasion of the world, they can help to maintain the dynamic equilibrium of life, can promote the renewing tension of hope, and teach the urgent lesson of joy in the midst of the struggle, since the eschatological time, the time of salvation, has already begun.

Translated by Paul Burns

Juan Martin Velasco

Movements of Religious Awakening in the History of Religions

MOVEMENTS of religious awakening form a particular category within the movements or reform that occur in all religions. All religions, in fact, show a similar profile of historical development. After their foundation, which constitutes a more or less violent break with an earlier religious tradition, and a charismatic early period of rapid expansion, they all become stabilized, organizing their original religious impetus into a more or less rigid institutional framework. The religious institution regulates and establishes the various social, cultic, rational and ethical expressions that had gone to make up the original religious ideal. The inevitable institutionalization of the religious ideal involves a series of consequences for the manner in which it is practised. Insistence on different institutional aspects of religious life frequently leads to its becoming formal and routine, generally through being reduced to a belief, to an acceptance of a set of established formulas for the truth in which faith (in a stricter or looser sense) has been expressed; through being reduced to the practice of a set of ritual or moral precepts; through external belonging to the society in which acceptance of the primitive ideal has become crystallized.

The history of all the great religions shows cases of reforming individuals or communities raising their voices against this systematization of religious life. Their history therefore contains an element intrinsic to religion itself, which brings about the processes of reform or revitalization, among which the movements of religious awakening are numbered.

Religion in its permanently institutionalized form also brings about a second set of consequences. The very permanence, and in particular the institutionalization of a religion, make it a major historical fact subject to all the sorts of vicissitudes through which human history itself must pass. The continual process of change in history cannot fail to influence religious life, incarnate as it is in an institutional body necessarily living in a particular age. So the very durability of religion will force a re-establishment of its institutional body whenever deep changes in historical circumstances make it impossible for its primitive ideal to be realized within the framework of an outworn institutional form. The necessary transformation of the institutional body will require a reformulation of the religious ideal embodied in it. So there is a particular reason—in some manner external to the religion itself—for the appearance of movements aiming at transforming the religious institution and the forms in which the ideal that inspires it are understood and lived.

I. Religious Awakening and Revitalization

Religious awakening is one of these movements. Although it appears in all religions at different moments in their history, it is not always easy to discern the features that distinguish it from any other series of events more or less closely linked with it. In my view, it belongs among those movements of revitalization that A. F. C. Wallace has defined as "a conscious, deliberate and organized effort by members of a society to bring about a more satisfactory culture".[1] In this case it would be an effort to bring about a more satisfactory form of religious expression and embodiment. In movements of revitalization it emerges clearly as an element of protest against the institutionalization of religion, set in motion by a new religious experience, more intense than that which has become crystallized in the institution, and by the conflict between this and new historical situations that have lessened its credibility. All these movements presuppose a sense of unease as their starting-point; they always arise at moments of

[1] "Revitalization Movements", in *American Anthropologist*, no. 58 (1958), p. 265.

crisis for the religious institution and the culture in which it exists, and all aspire to the instigation of a new way of life, or at least of a new organization that will allow the original ideal to flourish once more. All such movements, at least when their success corresponds to their original impetus, lead to the establishment of a new society, whose size and duration will vary with its success.

There are numerous religious phenomena in which these characteristics of movements of revitalization are present. Among them are to be found the various forms of religious awakening and reform, messianic, millennialist, "nativist", and so on. These movements are differentiated from each other by the presence in each of supplementary characteristics besides those we have distinguished as common to them all, or by different ways of displaying the common characteristics. The differences are often due to the particular religious context in which they arise. The best way to distinguish them would seem to be to pick out the characteristics that differentiate them from the other movements of revitalization closest to them.

II. Religious Awakening, Reforms and Nativisms

The common ground for all these movements is cultural and religious disquiet. In movements of religious awakening this disquiet is basically religious and is caused by the inability of the institution to satisfy the religious needs of its subjects, particularly those that make up the masses. The starting-point of a religious awakening is the situation of a group whose religious experience cannot be expressed within institutional channels that have become too formal, narrow or compromised with the dominant cultural situation.[2]

In movements of reform, on the other hand, the disquiet normally arises from the inability of institutionalized forms of religion to serve as a vehicle for religious life and experience in a

---

[2] R. A. Knox refers to this last aspect in his *Enthusiasm: A Chapter in the History of Religion with Special Reference to the XVIIth and XVIIIth Centuries* (Oxford, 1950), affirming that movements of enthusiasm, which are a sort of movement of revitalization, start from the suspicion that "a Church allied to the world has de-ecclesialized itself".

particular historical situation that shows them up as outmoded. In "Nativisms", or "religious movements of liberation and salvation of oppressed peoples",[3] the disquiet is produced above all by the oppression exercised on the very religious identity by cultural or religious systems, as the case may be, imposed in more less violent forms by the forces of colonialism or invasion.

This first difference in their starting-points leads straight to the different concepts of the new life that the various movements of revitalization aim to bring into being. Religious awakening tries to bring back the old, original form of religion, freed from its compromises with the successive cultures that have left their mark on the institutionalization of the original ideal. So it pays very little—if any—attention to the historical circumstances of the time in which it occurs. The original form becomes the one thing necessary that disqualifies all the achievements of progress.[4] This is why "revivalist" movements insist on the importance of piety and usually appear in the form of a sort of puritanism that rejects all the concessions of accommodation to the world, even when they appear in a clearly "a-nomist" guise.[5] Religious awakening is generally a backward-looking movement, trying to escape from its present situation and reverse the course of history to the zero point of the origin of the movement, the time of the birth of its religion.

Movements of reform also have an element of restoration in them, but tend to concentrate both on the original nucleus and on the transformation of the institution necessary for the original ideal to be lived at the time of the reform. "Nativisms" show a marked propensity to millennialism in the sense that they characterize the new situation they hope to bring about as a return to the golden age that existed before the situation of oppression in which they originate.

All movements of revitalization have a charismatic subject as their prime mover, though here again there are elements of dif-

---

[3] For a description of these movements, cf. V. Lanternari, *Movimenti religiosi di Libertà e di Salvezza dei Popoli oppressi* (Milan, 1960), and the bibliography contained therein.

[4] G. van der Leeuw, *La religion dans son essence et ses manifestations* (Paris, 1955), p. 600.

[5] R. A. Knox, *op. cit.*, p. 2.

ference between them. Promoters of religious awakening frequently appear to be in direct touch with the supernatural through visions, private revelations or special powers, but although the presence of a religious leader is a constant, the subjects of religious awakenings tend to be communities or groups rather than isolated individuals. The supernatural character of the leader is extended to the "revivalist" community, and all the members of the community will often be conscious of sharing, in a sort of common priesthood, the charisms that the hierarchy and clergy had reserved to themselves in the institutional stage.

In this sense, as van der Leeuw says, "religious awakening is a reform stemming from the experience of the masses, an experience of God coming alive in the bosom of the community".[6] So the subject of these movements is a community, generally small in numbers, which pays most attention to the guidance of the Spirit it experiences directly and therefore feels itself set apart from the institution from which it sprang, which it accuses of worldliness.[7] In movements of reform, on the other hand, rather than the community being the active agent, the initiative stems from an individual who realizes the inadequacy of a particular form of religion and proclaims the need for its renovation if religion can continue to be experienced by all. In nativisms the person who works the transformation frequently takes on the mythical characteristics of a messiah who comes from another world and makes the beginning of a new era possible.

The differences between the various kinds of movements of revitalization are reflected in the means each uses for the attainment of its ends. The predominantly communitary character of the movement of religious awakening makes it concentrate on emotive expression and an appeal to the senses as a vehicle of revitalization. "Revivalist" communities live in a constant state of contagious common enthusiasm, stemming from the Spirit with which they are in immediate contact. Their consciousness of this immediate contact often leads them into moods of ecstasy through which they express this direct relationship with the supernatural. Their religious experience is expressed informally, breaking with the forms hallowed by tradition, and enthusiasm

[6] *Op. cit.*, p. 599.   [7] R. A. Knox, *op. cit., passim.*

in worship is given preference over more sober aspects such as ethical behaviour or rational conceptualization. Their enthusiasm and consciousness of their direct communion with the supernatural usually gives revivalist movements a pronounced missionary character, which in the beginning leads to their rapid expansion.[8]

Nativisms, particularly when their roots are endogenous, that is, when they derive from the imbalance between institutional pressures imposed "from above" and the religious demands and needs of the people that the institution fails to satisfy, adopts the same sacral and cultural mode of expression as that of the revivalist movements, and are even more given, if possible, to the external and bodily expression—in song and dance, for example—of these forms of worship.

Reform movements, on the other hand, usually insist on the need to give religious expressions an ethical and spiritual content, and often move in the direction of reducing the outward show of forms of worship, the better to adapt it to the new historical situation. So preaching and the word acquire enhanced importance in reformed worship, as a means of bringing home to the individual the spiritual content of his religious actions.

Just as the means employed by the different forms of revivalist movement are different, so are the results they achieve. Religious awakening seems to bear most on transformation of the individual, renewal of his heart through intensification of his religious experience, and generally results in the emergence of a community set apart from the official community—though not necessarily officially detached from it—which comes to take on the usual characteristics of a sect—a break with institution and society, an insistence on religion as the only ordering principle in life, a strong sense of identity and a marked tendency to exclusivism. Reform, on the other hand, tends to concentrate more on transforming the existing structures, and so produces a new institution more in tune with the needs of the time, but which only in special circumstances breaks away from the parent institution. The reformed community is therefore more likely to last than the revivalist ones, and to be less markedly exclusive

[8] Warren, *Revival: an Enquiry* (London, 1954).

than the latter with their consciousness of direct communication with the Godhead. Nativist movements often result in the establishment of "churches" that express the immediate cultural needs of a people under colonialism and try to meet these needs with themes taken syncretically from both the native religious tradition and that of the colonizers. Such churches often take on the aspect of messianic and millenniary communities seeking a new age in which the complex situation of oppression that brought them into being will have disappeared.

The features enumerated so far enable us to define movements of religious awakening as a particular class of movements of revitalization. But none of the known historical movements will show all these features together, or at least not all to the same extent. On the other hand, the religious context and particular historical circumstances peculiar to each of these movements determine important features particular to them. So an attempt such as this at describing such movements should end with a description of some of the more important ones that have arisen in the course of the history of certain religions.

III. HASIDISM, A RELIGIOUS AWAKENING IN JUDAISM

The term *ḥāsîd* means pious, and so Hasidism can be considered as an analogous phenomenon to Christian pietism. It is now seen as a movement of "mystical revivalism" and "religious awakening" within Judaism.[9] Modern Hasidism started in the eighteenth century among the Jewish communities of Eastern Europe, particularly in Poland.[10] All the authorities are agreed that it arose out of a situation that had led these communities to an exceptional state of cultural, socio-economic and religious poverty within the country. The political instability of the country, and the poverty of the Jewish communities, especially in the South, together with other more specifically religious causes, such as the failure of the messianic sabbatial movement

---

[9] R. Schatz–Uffenheimer, "Self-redemption in Hasidic Thought", in *Types of Redemption*, ed. Werblowsky and Bleeker (Leiden, 1970), p. 207.
[10] For a description of Hasidism, cf. "Hasidism", in *The Jewish Encyclopedia*, vol. IV, pp. 251–6; "Chassidismus", in *Encyclopaedia Judaica*, vol. V, pp. 359–86; M. Buber, *Die Erzählungen der Chassidim* (Zürich, 1949), Introduction, pp. 15–110.

and other baptist movements of the time, resulted in a sense of disappointment, aided by the failure on the part of the rabbinical Judaism that held sway at the time to satisfy the spiritual and religious hunger of the lower echelons of the population.

The leader of the movement was Israel ben Eliezer, known as Baal Shem-tov (1700–1760), the possessor of a strongly charismatic personality, to whom miraculous powers of prophecy and healing were attributed, and who had the gift of understanding the needs of the masses and acting in accordance with them. It has been said of his movement that "from the start it sought ways to the people and spoke the language of the people".[11] In opposition to the rabbinical formalism and legalism of the epoch, and its insistence on doctrine, Hasidism stressed the need for revitalizing the faith of the believer, understood as a close relationship with the divinity, whose presence can be discerned in the whole of creation.

This insistence on faith as an attitude—Hasidism, it has been said, "tried to reform the believer, not the faith"—and on the closeness of God to the believer, shows itself in a religious practice marked by piety, fervour, enthusiasm and joy as basic attributes. Another characteristic of this Jewish pietism was the formation of numerous small communities based on the mutual love between their members gathered around the ṣaddiqim. "The communities of ḥasidim dependent on a ṣaqqid, particularly the narrow circle constantly in attendance upon him, seem to have formed a powerful dynamic unity."[12] The presence of the ṣaqqid and his role in the communities acquired an extraordinary importance; he was considered to possess all sorts of powers, was surrounded by all sorts of attentions, beginning with ministration to his material needs, and haloed with a proliferation of marvellous accounts of his life and miracles. The original Hasidism, the one that developed in South Poland under the aegis of Baal Shem-tov and Maggid of Mezerich, was also distinguished by its mystical tendencies, which have been called "spiritual introversion", as well as a distinct bias towards "passivity in relation to external historical events".[13] This has led to modern interpretations seeing it as a deviation from the classic Judaic preoccupation

---

[11] "Chassidismus", *art. cit.*, p. 383.   [12] M. Buber, *op. cit.*, p. 26.
[13] R. Schatz-Uffenheimer, *op. cit.*, p. 209.

with an historical process of redemption and as a tendency to "interiorization of spiritual renewal".

Hasidism's radical break with rabbinical Judaism earned it the decided opposition of the official ranks of the latter. It was branded an "atheist sect", its members were excommunicated, marriage with them forbidden, and funeral ceremonies denied them. Despite this, the communities' missionary zeal led to their rapid spread, particularly among the masses. Then during the nineteenth century, Hasidism had to contend with the currents of "illumined" Judaism, which dubbed it an obscurantist and reactionary sect. Despite this further opposition, Hasidism has continued in existence until our day and is considered one of the most important instances of revitalization of faith produced within Judaism.[14] It is also the only movement that, despite official opposition, has remained within the bosom of the Jewish faith and not cut itself off from the main body.[15]

IV. Movements of Religious Awakening and Reform in Modern Islam

The development of Islam in the past few centuries has been conditioned by a double movement of reform. The first aspect has been a reaction against the inner decadence of its religious institutions, affected as they were by the exuberant developments of medieval exegesis, by later degeneration and indifference and by a proliferation of superstitious popular practices. The second has been mainly a form of response to the impact made on the life of Islam by its confrontation with the modern world in the shape of Western colonialism. The response to this situation of oppression has, on the religious level, been chiefly along the lines of a return to primitive Islam, without the slightest compromise with the present historical situation, or alternatively, along the lines of an attempt to adapt the original principles of Islam to the changed conditions of the modern world. The first tendency has a clearly "revivalist" character—though tinged with the particular religious context of Islam—and its present-day exponent is the movement of *Wahabism*. The second contains all the elements of a movement of religious reform, and its principal ex-

---

[14] Buber, *op. cit.*, p. 28; "Chassidismus", p. 383.   [15] *Ibid.*

ponents are the various branches of the movement known as *salafiyya*. A comparison between the two can shed further light on the general phenomenon of religious awakening.

Wahabism originated as a movement of protest against the internal crisis that ran through Islam in the eighteenth century.[16] Its promoter, Muhammad Ibn Abd-el-Wahab (1703–1787), who lived in central Arabia, set out to renew Islam by shedding all the accretions that it had taken on over the centuries—whether the intellectualizing tendencies of the philosophers, the sentimental, interiorizing work of the mystics, or the superstitious character of popular religiosity. Faced with all these innovations, Wahabism proclaimed a return to the sources of primitive Islam in all its dogmatic, juridical and moral purity. This return to primitive Islam links Wahabism with the mediaeval reform of Ibn Taymiyya, and reaches back to the doctrine of the tradition stemming from Ibn Hambal, the pure doctrine of the "golden age" of Islam practised by Mahommed and put into effect by his companions. Its *'aqida*, or profession of faith, rejects as polytheism the extension to beings other than Allah of the veneration that belongs to him alone, including as veneration calling on them as intercessors; it calls all those who deny the determinism of human actions infidels, as well as those who use allegorical interpretation in exegesis of the Koran.

Together with this doctrinal purity, Wahabism requires a similar purification of religious practices, and inveighs against veneration of tombs and relics, the building of minarets next to mosques and everything that departs from the simplicity of the primitive period. The return to source is also seen in a rigorous opposition to the introduction of novelties such as coffee and tobacco, and upholds the application of the full rigour of the law against all who transgress its precepts. It has the strictest regard for the law, purifying it of all the additives of tradition, without the slightest concession to new circumstances or the least attention to the transformations wrought by the conditions of the modern world. In this context the following sentence from its *'aqida* is significant: "I confess that all novelty in religious

---

[16] For all the following part, cf. F. Pareja, *Islamología* (Madrid, 1952–4), pp. 608–11; R. Hartmann, "Die Wahhabiten", in *Zeitschrift für Deutschen Morgenländischen Gesellschaft*, no. 78 (1924), pp. 176–213.

matters is modernism.''[17] Such a total rejection of all novelties leads it to reject not a few points admitted by the common consent of the doctors of the community, the *igma'*, and to proclaim its own right to examine the sources of Islam according to the lights of its own reasoning. "It obeys the original law in its entirety, unconditionally, and only it, and establishes a society in which this law is to be held in respect." For Wahabism this is Islam and all the rest is superfluous and false.[18] So it is not surprising that the movement has been called "Islamic Puritanism".[19]

This revivalism of the origins has nothing romantic in its approach, however. Ibn Abd-el-Wahab used all the means at his command to instigate his new society, and his aims were accomplished by winning the Emir Muhammad Ibn Sa'ūd to his cause; he propagated the new movement by force of arms until—after many setbacks—it covered the extensive territories that now make up Saudi Arabia. Naturally, the movement encountered armed resistance, and its doctrines were declared heretical on account of the break with the official Islamic community. But its clear affirmation of a pure religious ideal had a considerable influence on the later reform movements that are grouped together under the heading of *salafiyya*, and so it can still be considered to survive to this day.

Salafiyya is also, as the name indicates, a return to the Islam of the *salaf*, to the first antecedents, and to the Koran freed from the dead weight of the interpretations of later schools. But this return is not only a response to the internal decadence of Islam, it arises also from the need, and the will, to adapt it to the new conditions of the modern world. So these movements are not an affair of blind return to an unchangeable past, but of adaptation of the essential religious nucleus of Islam to the new historical situation. Their representatives are therefore aiming at a transformation of the institution of Islam rather than at a restoration of an earlier form of it. In this sense they are true movements of reform rather than "revivalist" movements or movements of religious awakening. *Salafiyya*, as represented above all by

[17] Hartmann, *art. cit.*, p. 183.
[18] W. C. Smith, *Islam in Modern History* (London, 1957).
[19] Van der Leeuw, *op. cit.*, p. 600, n. 1.

Muhammad 'Abdub (d. 1905), does not passively accept the legal dispositions that regulate the life of the Muslim as immutable norms valid for all time, but recognizes the historical conditioning of their formulation and tries to bring the precepts contained in the Koran up to date. It is opposed to a fatalistic interpretation of submission to the will of Allah, stressing, on the contrary, that the will of Allah is that Muslims should show themselves as active, progressive and constant as the prophet himself was. These reformers distinguish purely religious precepts from those related to the temporal order and so open the way to the relative autonomy of science, philosophy and the political structure of the community.

Once this distinction has been made, they subject those precepts dependent on the temporal order to major changes in accordance with the new situation, without sacrificing their principle. In order to effect this change they usually appeal to the principle of rational examination of the texts and traditions, *igtihād*, which has always existed in Islam. All these renovatory principles have made the modernization of Islam possible. But the representatives of the *salafiyya*, and particularly Muhammad 'Abdub, ally these principles to strict religious adherence to the religious principles of Islam together with a parallel modern interpretation of them. This is what distinguishes the reforming current from other currents that break from traditional Islam and become reduced to purely nationalist movements.[20]

V. Conclusions

Movements of religious awakening arise at a moment in the history of religions characterized by excessive institutionalization of the religious impulse and by a critical situation in the religions or cultures in which they are produced. The permanent conjuncture of such conditions indicates that these movements, far from being a "closed chapter in the history of religions", represent a permanent possibility within them. Furthermore, the present circumstances of an accelerating rate of change in struc-

[20] F. Pareja, *op. cit.*, pp. 621 ff. On Muslim reform movements cf. also Elie Salem, "Arab Reformers and the Reinterpretation of Islam", in *The Muslim World*, Oct. 1955, pp. 311–20.

tures, the current multiplicity of religions and the growing points of contact between different cultures make it likely that their incidence will increase rather than decrease.[21]

Religious awakening provides an opportunity for revitalizing religion, and for the intensification of religious experience in particular. But its marked tendency to attempt to restore earlier attitudes and its slight, or non-existent, attention to current circumstances in which this experience has to be lived appear to condemn it to a marginal existence parallel to the real march of events, to a remoteness from the centre and to a tendency to escape from reality, which will inevitably considerably reduce its effectiveness and compromise its future, condemning it to appear as purely utopian and lacking in effective transcendence.

Yet, despite these real dangers, movements of religious awakening have undeniably contributed to the enrichment and renewal of the religions in which they have emerged. They are in large measure to be thanked for the fact that, despite the institutional tendency to reduce religious life to a routine, it has constantly risen again from the "splendid tomb" of the institution in which it has so often tried to bury itself. Revival movements have often provided reform movements with the attention to purely religious experience needed for them to avoid the danger of reducing religion to ethics, politics or philosophy. And to the extent that they themselves have paid attention to the institutional aspects of religion and to the historical circumstances that surround them, to the extent to which they have enriched themselves with reforming elements, that is, they have probably provided one reason for regarding the future of religion in our time with hope.

Translated by Paul Burns

[21] It is not difficult to find reactions similar to those traced in Islamism in modern Hinduism, faced with the internal decadence of the religion itself and the shock of contact with Western culture. H. Glasenapp, *Religiöse Reformbewegungen im Heutigen Indien* (Leipzig, 1928), studies five reform movements and contains an interesting description of the five main forms taken by reforming activity. The movement known as Arya-Samaj, led by Dayanand Sarasvati and called by Glasenapp, "a new awakening of the Vedic religion", would seem to come closest to what I have characterized as a movement of religious awakening, even taking into account the number of features specific to the Hindu context in which it arose.

Günter Remmert

Spiritual Movements and Political Praxis

"WHEN examined from the point of view of the part it plays in socializing the individual or in consolidating society, religion can appear either as a stabilizing or as an emancipating factor. Its influence... is sometimes reactionary, sometimes progressive. Historical and critical research shows that religion sometimes effected progress in the political realization of human freedom, but in innumerable other cases completely thwarted it."[1]

I. Conflicting Interpretations

As soon as charismatic movements inside and outside the major Christian denominations began to arouse attention in the last few decades, they met a crossfire of criticism. Apart from the theological and intra-denominational controversies which they provoked, it was their social and political significance that was chiefly discussed. Two main evaluations emerged.

The verdict that religiously motivated charismatic movements were both in aim and in practical effect completely unpolitical is one of these two evaluations and possibly the most widely accepted one. These movements, it is argued, are only concerned with a spiritual experience within the individual—something far removed from harsh political realities. The adherents of such groups, so it is said, put more trust in vague emotions and uncertain intuitions than in rational insight and argument. If they

[1] H.-E. Bahr, Preface to K.-W. Dahm, N. Luhmann, D. Stoodt, *Religion—System und Sozialisation* (Darmstadt and Neuwied, 1972), p. 7.

ever ventured into the political arena, their efforts had little effect. Their ethical strictness permitted no compromises and soon turned into resignation.

The starting-point or tacit basis of this evaluation is often the idea that politics take primacy over other fields of activity. The criterion employed in this judgment is to inquire about direct political work, public attitudes, individual actions, and so forth. The verdict of the left-wing socialist L. Pestalozza on the Italian Pentecostal movement will serve as a representative example of this view: "The Pentecostalists have no constructive alternative to the present organization of society; they comfort themselves for the trials of this world with the certainty of happiness in another world. Mystical participation in the religious life of the community and reading the Gospel do not solve any human problems; the most they can do is to dull them by the willing acceptance of suffering."[2]

The opposite view is often held by members of charismatic groups themselves. They assert that their movement has considerable political influence and fulfils an indispensable function in society. What stimulates social and political progress, they say, is the furtherance of central moral values at a clear distance from day-to-day political life with its struggles for power. Only religious motives can guarantee clear insights which subsequently influence praxis. In an age in which ethics have been driven out of politics, it is precisely charismatic movements which must give politics fresh validity.

The starting-point or tacit basis of this evaluation is often the idea that the religious realm takes primacy over others. Confronted with this or that activity, those who hold this view inquire about the moral and religious convictions of the person responsible and evaluate his activity accordingly. Thus in 1958 the Pentecostal preacher R. Willenegger drew up for the Swiss national elections a manifesto which included the following statement: "On list 7 you choose men who are concerned about the moral state of our people. Materialism, criminality, embezzlement, divorce, robbery with violence, suicide, and so on, have

[2] L. Pestalozza, "Il diritto di non tremolare, La condizione delle minoranze religiose in Italia", *L'Attualità*, 14 (Milan and Rome, 1956); quoted in W. J. Hollenweger (Ed.), *Die Pfingstkirchen* (Stuttgart, 1971), p. 329.

reached a stage that threatens to sap the moral fibre of our country.... On list 7 you choose men who are convinced that without God's protecting hand the military defence of our country would be founded on sand. It is time for the spiritual defence of the country; it is time for reverence for God's name, a return to the demands of the Bible, prayers for the defence of our frontiers and pledges for the maintenance and consolidation of peace on earth."[3] Which of the two verdicts is appropriate? Or are they not after all mutually exclusive, as one might at first suppose?

Outbursts of enthusiasm in Christianity are not a twentieth-century novelty. It is possible to judge historical developments from a distance in time that does not distort the proportions too much. But before we attempt to test the political effectiveness or ineffectiveness of such groups by the historical facts, let us glance briefly at the political and social conditions that produce them.

II. CONDITIONS WHICH PRODUCE REVIVALIST GROUPS

In a state in which church life flourishes and social conditions satisfy everyone, revivalist movements are unlikely to occur. The opposite must be the case. When the traditional churches no longer fill certain religious needs or seem not to fill them, a group of people with the same spiritual experiences, and often with a strong collective feeling of "conversion", will draw away more or less explicitly from the Church and from a community that demands a more intensive religious commitment and promises a more deeply felt satisfaction.

Both when Methodism arose in England in the eighteenth century and later during the Réveil in France and Holland the charismatics cut themselves off from the established Protestant Church, whose rites had become sterile and whose institutions had become an end in themselves. Nor would the following of the Pentecostal Movement in this century have grown so quickly if the big Christian churches had not lost so much of their power to persuade and influence people.

But alongside the ecclesiastical situation social and political

[3] Quoted in Hollenweger, op. cit., pp. 356–7.

conditions also play an important part. This is shown by the participation of certain strata of the population in the revivalist movement and the swift spread of such movements in times of cultural change. Research indicates, for example, that in the initial stages of Pentecostal movements low-income groups are particularly strongly represented. In the U.S.A. socially deprived negro sections of the population and in Chile poverty-stricken natives are specially susceptible to the appeal of these movements.

Thus a considerable proportion of the adherents consists of people not very well off materially and neglected socially who are obliged to suffer economic exploitation, discrimination and lack of any political representation. The revivalist movement promises them liberation from this miserable situation. At community meetings social barriers are lowered, the isolation of one person from another is eliminated, each helps and respects the other. Whether this liberation has any political effect outside the limits of the community needs more careful examination.

III. DIFFERING ATTITUDES TO POLITICS

In any case, the political attitude of a charismatic group depends on the ecclesiastical and political conditions in which it arises. In addition to these two factors there are the influences from other realms of the socio-cultural context, influences which in certain circumstances can modify considerably the social and political commitment. These influences make it impossible to relate the political practice of a group solely to its religious views.[4]

Do charismatic communities endorse the existing social and political conditions or do they call them into question? Does their criticism, assuming it is present, also act as an influence for change? Basically, three types of attitude to politics seem possible:

1. The political forces in a state and the charismatic minority are intent on keeping their distance from each other. The charismatic movement renounces any kind of political activity.

[4] Cf. H. P. Dreitzel (Ed.), *Sozialer Wandel* (Neuwied and Berlin, 1967).

2. The religious minority endorses and supports the prevailing political forces. Its commitment can go as far as defending existing political conditions against criticism and resisting any change.

3. Charismatic groups welcome and support social changes, if indeed they do not initiate them. They help with both theoretical and practical work to carry out these changes and put them into effect.

I shall now try to give concrete examples of this type of political practice by means of historical examples from the revival movement of the eighteenth and nineteenth centuries in Protestant territory[5] and from the Pentecostal movement of the twentieth century.[6]

IV. THE NEUTRAL POSITION

1. *The* Réveil *in France—in Favour of Separation of Church and Politics*

An example of the strict division of spheres of influence on the basis of a more or less friendly coexistence of the political forces with the religious minority is provided by the French *Réveil*, a Protestant revival movement at the beginning of the nineteenth century. A decisive influence on this movement was exerted by Adolphe Monod (1802–1863) and his brother Frédéric (1794–1863). They attacked the dead ecclesiasticism and petrified orthodoxy of official Protestantism and insisted on personal conversion and the public confession of faith. Like many revival movements, the *Réveil* is characterized by a legalistic ethic and strict belief in the Bible.

The revivalists did not venture on any involvement in social and political questions. This followed logically from their conviction that the state church was irreconcilable with the essential nature of religion. Their mission chapels with the inscription "Church not paid by the State" attracted a large number of people.

[5] E. Beyreuther, "Die Erweckungsbewegung", in *Die Kirche in ihrer Geschichte*, ed. by K. D. Schmidt and E. Wolf (Göttingen, 1963).
[6] W. J. Hollenweger, *Enthusiastisches Christentum* (Wuppertal and Zürich, 1969); *idem, Die Pfingstkirchen* (Stuttgart, 1971).

However, against the background of the pressing problems of the French working classes it can only be regretted that the ministers and adherents of the *Réveil* had little understanding of the economic and social distress of large sections of the population. The only exception was S. Vincent (1787–1837), who in spite of his commitment to the *Réveil* was critical of it because of its narrow dogmatism. For example, he made energetic efforts to get the standard of teaching in primary schools raised and methods of cultivation improved and refused to be discouraged by the opposition of reactionary circles. The other notable figures in the movement paid no attention to social morality or to co-operation in public life.

2. *The Church of God (Cleveland, U.S.A.)—Unburdening the Soul in Social Struggles*

While the adherents of the French *Réveil* came mainly from the lower middle classes, examples from the Pentecostal movement of the twentieth century show that social commitment need not necessarily be present even when a large proportion of the membership consists of people from socially deprived sections of the population.

L. Pope has analysed the attitude of the Church of God, Cleveland, an American Pentecostal church, during the textile workers' strike at Gastonia (New Haven, Conn.) in the thirties. His investigations suggest that the traditional churches made no effort at all to cope with the situation. The lack of solidarity with the textile workers was bound to have a detrimental affect and benefited the Pentecostal movement. The latter, it is true, took no social or political action, but did feel at one with the strikers. This explains its swift growth at the expense of the traditional churches, to which eighty per cent of the members of Pentecostal groups had previously belonged. Pope's diagnosis of the rapid growth was as follows:

"Frenetic religious services make the participants feel relief from the psychological pressure. They find it possible to express their ego in a way that they need to and can identify with a great power that is on their side. ... The unusually high percentage of women, who seem to be most active in the semi-hysterical religious practices, is significant. Seventy-five per cent of the members of the Church of God in Gastonia were women."[7]

Such observations are only confirmed by a sociological survey made in the U.S.A. in 1936. This indicates that the Pentecostalists were strongest in the southern states. There were more women than men in each community and more blacks than whites. The average income of members of Pentecostal communities was considerably lower than that of members of American parishes as a whole, and lower even than that of purely negro parishes.[8]

This characteristic only remains true up to about the Second World War. Since then a rise in the social scale has considerably altered the sociological composition of the Church of God. W. J. Hollenweger, the historian of the Pentecostal movement, comes to this conclusion:

"The hope . . . that the Pentecostal communities could give the negroes more than human warmth, joyful religious services and spontaneous human assistance, that they would stand by them in their struggle for recognition as human beings with full human rights, has been disappointed. We have to resign ourselves today to noting that the American Pentecostal movement has abandoned the important role it could have assumed in the struggle of the American churches in favour of membership of the bourgeois National Association of Evangelicals, a body which is politically and theologically conservative."[9]

3. Pentecostalists in Chile—the Small Protective Society

The decision which political tendency the Pentecostalists should embrace does not yet seem to have been made in Africa and Latin America. Some of the indigenous Pentecostal churches there voted for membership of the World Council of Churches, because they hoped for support in their recognition of their social and political responsibility. But their task seems to be perceived so far only by a minority, as can be seen from the example of Chile.

The Chilean Pentecostal movement split off in 1910 from the

[7] L. Pope, Millhands and Preachers (Yale, ⁴1958), p. 135. Quoted in Hollenweger, Enthusiastisches Christentum, op. cit., p. 62.
[8] Hollenweger, Enthusiastisches Christentum, op. cit., p. 27.
[9] Hollenweger, Die Pfingstkirchen, op. cit., p. 20.

Methodist mother church and founded the Iglesia Metodista
Pentecostal. From the start the direction was assumed by natural
leaders of individual groups. The result was a small, hierarchi-
cally organized but classless society, in which everyone possesses
the same opportunities at the start. The Pentecostal community
offers its members the protection of a fraternal partnership and
a recognized status defined by the interplay of definite rights and
duties, with the latter often seen as privileges. Human relationships are governed by mutual help and support of the sick and
unemployed. The minister, who combines some of the characteristics of father and employer, plays the part of initiator as well
as leader.

D'Epinay attributes to the Chilean Pentecostal movement a
basically apolitical attitude.[10] In his view it abolishes the theological tension between the present and future kingdoms of God and
concentrates on a kingdom beyond this world. This leads it to
behave like an ideology of order, which neither initiates nor
supports social changes. The price of this renunciation of a critical attitude to the present organization of society is a largely un-
conscious appropriation of values and patterns of behaviour from
the stratum of society immediately above one's own.

V. A Stabilizing Force

1. *Pentecostalists in the Eastern Bloc—Participants in Building Socialism*

In the present Eastern bloc there is a whole series of charismatic groups, which deliberately keep away from any political
activity that aims at making changes. Not without reason, they
fear a worsening of relations with the socialist state, which allows
them some scope for activity, if not very much. In order to retain
this scope, the charismatic minority takes pains to keep affirming
its loyalty to official positions.

To assess this attitude correctly we must remind ourselves of
the historical development of these groups. In Romania, for example, the community, which came into being in 1922, soon had
to suffer from the trickery of the authorities. Various attempts

[10] C. L. D'Epinay, *El Refugio de las Masas* (Santiago de Chile, 1968).

to secure public recognition failed and the persecution reached its climax in 1940–44 under Antonescu's regime. The organizational apparatus was destroyed and the separate communities were isolated from each other; however, it proved impossible to root out the movement itself. When the Hitler regime was overthrown and the state terror stopped, it is estimated that the Penecostalists still numbered some 20,000.

Since then, the Pentecostalists in Romania seem to be content with the religious freedom granted to them. In 1950 the biggest group, the "Apostolic Pentecostal Church of God", centred in Arad, was fully recognized by the government of the Romanian People's Republic and given parity with the other religions. Since that time the Pentecostalists have pointed repeatedly to the harmonious relationship between Church and State in Romania. The chief editor of the only Pentecostal periodical in the country is never tired of making statements like this:

"Loyalty to the state is regarded by the Pentecostalists as a sacred law, laid down in Scripture in the words of the Apostle Paul: 'Remind them to be submissive to rulers and authorities, to be ready for any honest work' (Tit. 3. 1)."[11]

Similar attitudes are also characteristic of Poland. Here the Pentecostalists did have their own "parishes" until 1947 but they regarded themselves as part of the Lutheran Church. With the practice of adult baptism and the missionary activity of Polish emigrants returning from the U.S.A., there arose new communities, independent of each other, which combined after the Second World War mainly in the "United Evangelical Church". This was recognized by the state and its rights and duties laid down by statute.

The Pentecostalists in Poland, too, attach great importance to loyalty to the state authorities. In their view, Romans 13 and 1 Timothy 2 show that support of worldly authority is sanctioned by the Bible. E. Czajko, the deputy general secretary of the "United Evangelical Church", writes:

"Our church is loyal to the world authorities because they have created better opportunities for it to develop than existed in the period between the two wars. This loyalty is on the one

---

[11] Quoted in Hollenweger, *Die Pfingstkirchen, op. cit.*, p. 89.

hand the product of sound common sense but on the other hand it is also based on the teaching of Scripture."[12]

2. *Revival in Holland—the Struggle against Liberation and Revolution*

The stabilization of prevailing social conditions by revival movements is not a purely twentieth-century phenomenon. This is attested by an example from the Holland of the decades after the French Revolution. Here amidst violent political disputes the leading personalities of the revival movement in the Dutch Reformed Church took a very clear stand. In the person of the movement's founder, W. Bilderdijk (1756–1831), conservatism of an Orange, monarchical kind allied itself with orthodox Calvinism. Bilderdijk saw himself as a prophet in the Old Testament sense. In his eyes, political and religious conservatism were identical with the idea of good or of the Kingdom of God. The satanical opposing force bore the name "Revolution".

The year 1823 saw the appearance of Bilderdijk's pamphlet, "Complaints against the Spirit of the Century". In this pamphlet he sharply criticized, among other things, the decline of orthodox Calvinism, the new ideas of tolerance and humanity, the abolition of slavery (which is prescribed, he asserts, by Genesis 9. 25), paper constitutions, the elimination of the privileges of the nobility, the freedom of the press, the Code of Napoleon and all the "humbug about doing good".

VI. ATTEMPTS AT SOCIAL REFORMS—METHODISTS IN ENGLAND

Evidence of efforts by revival movements to change social conditions is not very often to be found, but occurs earliest in the Anglo-Saxon countries. A good example is the charismatic movement which led in eighteenth-century England, under the guidance of the Wesley brothers and Whitefield, to Methodism. Against the background of an Anglican Church which had sunk very low spiritually, passionate sermons calling for repentance, public conversions and confessions of faith had a swift and wide effect.

[12] Quoted in Hollenweger, *Die Pfingstkirchen, op. cit.*, pp. 93–4.

The "Test" oath demanded by the state church made the Methodist Nonconformists into adherents of parties favouring political reform. One of the results was the development in independent clubs of a movement for practical Christianity which was amazingly effective in the social life of a Great Britain in the process of moving over from cottage industries to factory techniques. Not only did the Wesleys succeed in uniting the miners in solid communities, but John Howard (1726–90) initiated humanitarian reforms in the prisons, Elizabeth Fry (1780–1845) did much, in the same field, for the improvement of the life of female prisoners, and Robert Raikes (1735–1811) started Sunday schools for the neglected young people of London.

Finally, William Wilberforce (1759–1833) became the leader of a movement for the abolition of slavery. He saw himself as "the tool in God's hand entrusted with effecting one of the greatest revolutions in the history of human society".[18] In 1807 he succeeded in having the slave trade made illegal for all English subjects and in 1834 the freeing of all slaves became a reality.

The mobilization of the laity in particular and extensive social activity based on the principles of the gospel prevented Socialism and Christianity from coming into fatal conflict with each other as they did on the Continent.

VII. Characteristics of Political Praxis

Let us return to our point of departure. Can one reproach revival moments in general with acting unpolitically or is it impossible to deny that they have exerted a certain degree of political influence? Do they help to consolidate political and social conditions or do they contribute to altering them? The historical material we have examined shows that both the evaluations described at the beginning of this article must be corrected. The verdict that these movements are completely unpolitical in both aim and actual effect calls for the following comments:

1. Charismatic movements are politically ambiguous phenomena.

[18] Quoted in H. Hermelink, *Das Christentum in der Menschheitsgeschichte*, I (Stuttgart and Tübingen, 1951), p. 262.

As the quotation from H.-E. Bahr at the beginning of this article suggests, one cannot predict what political line they will take. Their attitude seems to depend more on other circumstances than their own spirituality, although this is not without significance. Among these other factors are the social status of their adherents, the political attitude of other organizations, with which they can either co-operate or compete, educational influences, the political and economic interests of leading members, and so on.

2. In their modes of worship and in their community life, in which social differences are levelled out, and also in their chiliastic and utopian concepts, which anticipate a more just organization of society, revival movements are potentially critical of the social conditions prevailing at any given time.

3. The social work of the Methodists in England shows that a charismatic religious attitude can certainly be combined with a reforming social activity that goes beyond charitable help for individuals. Besides the work for certain socially deprived strata of the population, there is for example the commitment to the cause of peace (refusal to serve in the armed forces, service as mediators, and so on), which would merit an investigation of its own.

However, the second of the two judgments, which ascribes important political influence to revival movements, must also be modified.

1. To what extent moral values, on which charismatic groups lay great emphasis, influence political life is very difficult to determine. But this influence is much slighter than many revivalists assume.

2. Religious ideas can both help and hinder progress. Very often revival movements have refrained from taking part in politics. Most of their energies were spent on building up their own communities and on missionary activity; they had no strength left for social work.

3. There is also an obstacle on the theoretical side: whatever criticism of existing social conditions may be present takes the

form of imagining religious Utopias or even of entertaining chiliastic expectations.[14] The translation into a real Utopia, a step which could have consequences for political practice, never takes place. Chiliastic and utopian ideas, as anticipations of a just organization of life which cannot in present circumstances be achieved, certainly indicate some positive content in revivalists' thinking, but they provide no clue how this just social order is to be attained.

VIII. CONCLUSION

Whether or not charismatic movements will also remain apolitical in the future depends on the translation of charismatic ideas into a social ethic and a political programme which can only be pursued by rational methods. Must an initially genuine spiritual revival always be purchased at the cost of the renunciation of any attempt at the renewal of an important dimension of human life? It can only be hoped that present and future upsurges of enthusiasm in Christianity will not remain imprisoned in the one-dimensionality of their own spirituality. Some charismatic groups seem to have recognized the problem.[15] But recognizing a problem is by no means the same thing as solving it.

Translated by J. R. Foster

[14] Cf. A. Neusüss (Ed.), *Utopie* (Neuwied and Berlin, 1968).
[15] Cf. *New Covenant*, Oct.–Nov. 1972.

PART II
BULLETINS

Donald Gelpi

American Pentecostalism

ANY discriminating approach to American Pentecostalism must begin by distinguishing denominational Pentecostalism from neo-Pentecostalism. Denominational Pentecostalism began in 1900 at the Bethel Healing Home in Topeka, Kansas. It fused with revivalism to produce the Holiness Movement. And it has generated a bewildering variety of Pentecostal denominations.[1]

Denominational Pentecostalism tends towards theological fundamentalism. It affirms the infallibility of Scripture, the priesthood of the faithful and justification by faith. Its piety is also coloured by the emotionalism and rhetoric of the revivalist tradition.

American neo-Pentecostalism is by contrast an amorphous and free-wheeling phenomenon. It cannot be identified with any one denomination or credal position. It exists both within the traditional institutional churches and in informal extra-ecclesiastical groupings. It has given rise to interfaith Pentecostal organizations. It is doctrinally pluralistic. And it gives signs of becoming increasingly self-reflective and theologically sophisticated.

The Catholic charismatic renewal can be seen as one movement within the complex phenomenon of American neo-Pentecostalism. The Catholic movement is historically significant as the first popular revival of religion in the American mode in which the American Roman Catholic community has partici-

[1] J. Hardon, *The Protestant Churches of America* (New York, 1969), pp. 168–85; F. Bruner, *A Theology of the Holy Spirit* (Grand Rapids, 1970); J. Nichol, *Pentecostalism* (New York, 1966).

pated. And it promises to have significant impact on Catholic religious attitudes in the United States.[2]

In this essay, I would like to focus upon American neo-Pentecostalism as the more interesting and ecumenically promising of the two forms of American Pentecostalism. And I would like to reflect in particular upon the possible light which neo-Pentecostal piety throws upon Catholic sacramental theology.

I. THE SHARED TRAITS OF NEO-PENTECOSTAL PIETY

The most obvious trait that neo-Pentecostals of different American denominations have in common is that they come together regularly to pray. More important than the physical act of gathering, however, are the attitudes and expectations which are brought to the prayer meeting. For these condition both the structure of the meeting and the kind of experience they mediate.

Neo-Pentecostals come together to "focus on the Lord". All prayer is, of course, a focusing upon God. But in neo-Pentecostal piety one focuses on the Lord with the expectation that God will manifest himself visibly in the spontaneous activity of those who gather together to pray.[3]

It is this expectation which demands that the prayer meetings remain relatively unstructured. The group gathers to listen together to the Lord and to share in prayer whatever inspirations he gives them. One worshipper may feel moved to read a passage from Scripture which has spoken to him personally. Another may feel moved to testify to some favour, grace, insight, or divine healing. Another will be moved to exhort the group or to offer some teaching. But even these more "pedestrian" forms of sharing are interpreted as coming from the Lord since they proceed from an openness to the Spirit and to his inspirations.

As a result the atmosphere created at the prayer meetings is enormously supportive of and conducive to public sharing of often intimate and deeply personal religious experiences.

[2] E. O'Connor, The Pentecostal Movement in the Catholic Church (Notre Dame, 1971); D. Gelpi, Pentecostalism: A Theological Viewpoint (New York, 1971); Pentecostal Piety (New York, 1972); J. Ford, The Spirit and the Human Person (Dayton, 1969); The Pentecostal Experience (New York, 1970).

[3] J. Cavnar, Prayer Meetings (Pecos, New Mexico, 1969); J. Ford, "Spontaneous Prayer Meetings", Sisters Today, 41 (1970), pp. 342-7.

A further expectation of neo-Pentecostal prayer gatherings is that the charismatic gifts of prophecy and of tongues will also be present and operative at the meetings.

The scepticism of prophecy and tongues which one sometimes encounters among American Catholics is variously motivated. Sometimes it is symptomatic of the traditional hostility of the immigrant American Church to anything that smacks of Protestantism, especially fundamentalistic Protestant piety. But more often, perhaps, it is rooted in the prevailing rationalistic scepticism of unusual religious experiences that has traditionally characterized American secular culture since the days of Benjamin Franklin.

But among American Catholics there are also theological roots to such sceptical attitudes. On the relatively rare occasions when American Catholics reflect at all on the meaning of prophecy, they are apt to do so in very traditional scholastic categories. They will tend to assimilate prophecy to the higher graces of mystical prayer and to assume, as a result, that such gifts are granted only to exceptional saints, not to ordinary Christians. When joined to a "scientific" rationalism in religious matters, such notions can provide most ordinary Catholics with an easy rationalization for rejecting the "prophetic" claims of charismatics as symptomatic either of psychosis or of spiritual pride.

In point of fact, however, the experience of prophecy in charismatic prayer meetings bears little resemblance to extraordinary mystical grace, although it is rooted in a prayer experience. For the American neo-Pentecostal, the prophet is one who feels moved to speak some word to a specific community or individual. The word spoken is one of comfort, exhortation, warning, promise. It is spoken because the prophet feels in prayer that the Lord wishes the individual or community in question to hear such a word. And in well-ordered prayer groups, the prophecy is offered to the community and its leaders for prayerful discernment of its authenticity. Often during a prayer meeting, the word of prophecy will speak directly to the heart of the group as a whole. In such instances, it tends to evoke a confirmatory exclamation of praise and thanksgiving.

The experience of tongues is also frequently misunderstood and misinterpreted as a result of factual and theological misconceptions. There have been claims among neo-Pentecostals, both Catholic and Protestant. that the tongues spoken by charismatics are foreign languages, complete with vocabulary and syntax. Such an interpretation of the gift inclines one to regard the "interpretation" of tongues as something akin to a gift of translation. Were the experience of glossolalia and its interpretation anything of the sort it would truly verge on the miraculous. But the best linguistic studies of glossolalia indicate that the tongues spoken by neo-Pentecostals are not languages in the strict sense of the term. They do not give evidence of possessing systematic vocabulary and syntax.

As William Samarin puts it: "There is no mystery about glossolalia. Tape-recorded samples are easy to obtain and analyse. They always turn out to be the same thing: strings of syllables, made up of sounds taken from among all those that the speaker knows, put together more or less haphazardly but which nevertheless emerge as word-like and sentence-like units because of realistic, language-like rhythm and melody.... Yet in spite of superficial similarities, glossolalia is fundamentally not language. All specimens of glossolalia that have ever been studied have produced no features that would even suggest that they reflect some kind of communicative system." Samarin concludes that the chief significance of glossolalia is the fact that it is "a linguistic symbol of the sacred".[4]

Speaking in tongues among American Pentecostalism conforms to Samarin's description. It occurs either as an individual or as a group phenomenon. The syllables formed are either spoken or sung. Singing in tongues is in fact more clearly expressive of the basic neo-Pentecostal experience of glossolalia, for it is obviously a prayer of praise. But if Samarin is correct, then the interpretation of tongues must mean something less than strict linguistic translation. Glossolalia may be anomalous behaviour, but it is not an extraordinary gift (it is quite common); nor is it miraculous.

Neo-Pentecostals also pray often at prayer gatherings for con-

[4] W. Samarin, *Tongues of Men and Angels* (New York, 1970), pp. 227–9; M. Kelsey, *Tongue Speaking: an Experiment in Spiritual Experience* (New York, 1964); F. Goodman, *Speaking in Tongues: A Cross-Cultural Study of Glossolalia* (Chicago, 1972).

crete persons and intentions in an expectant faith that God will respond to their prayer in a visible and concrete way. If the individual prayed for is present the group will frequently gather round as a sign of concern and faith, and touch him or those nearest him.

Finally, both organized and spontaneous hymn-singing are integral to American neo-Pentecostal prayer. The song is, moreover, itself a prayer.

It should be clear from the above description that American neo-Pentecostal piety is characterized by the concreteness of its faith expectancy. The informal structure of the shared act of prayer is itself expressive of the expectation that when two or three are gathered in Jesus' name he will indeed make his presence felt by inspiring concrete individuals to perform specific religiously significant actions. The high premium placed upon petitionary prayer and on praise of God for his presence expresses the same concrete faith expectancy.

American neo-Pentecostal prayer is also characterized by the importance it places upon the sharing of religious feelings and experiences. It is assumed that such sharing should be accepted as part of the normal pattern of spiritual growth and development. It is also assumed that the expression of religious feeling is integral to human worship.

This free sharing and the concreteness of charismatic faith expectancy combine to mediate a felt sense of the worshipping community as a theophany, a quasi-sacramental revelation of the saving power and presence of the Spirit of Jesus.

These same religious attitudes usually combine to produce a spontaneous desire for sound teaching, leadership, and discernment in the prayer community. Where the expression of faith is devoid of personal feeling, there is little or nothing for anyone to discern; for discernment deals primarily with feelings and spontaneous impulses. But the discernment of spirits becomes imperative as soon as individuals or groups begin to take seriously the possibility that the concrete feelings which come in prayer can be inspired by the Holy Spirit. Such an expectation is, however, ascetically sound.

Moreover, as charismatic prayer communities grow, there usually develops a corresponding felt need for some individual or group of individuals to assume a leadership role in the discernment process. Especially in large groups it is often humanly impossible for the entire group to pray its way to unanimity on every practical question that confronts it.

Particularly in charismatic communities from a rich theological tradition, the vivid experiences had in prayer evoke a spontaneous desire for sound teaching. Often such experiences are sufficiently moving, even overwhelming, that they demand some kind of intelligible explanation. And where the experiences in question mediate a felt sense of the power and presence of God mere psychological explanations will not do.

Among American neo-Pentecostals the desire for doctrinal instruction will, of course, vary with membership. Among Catholic charismatics, the national leadership has placed a high premium on sound doctrinal instruction. And the American bishops have encouraged priests to become involved in Catholic groups in order to provide the needed teaching and pastoral guidance. To date, not enough priests have responded.[5]

But at the heart of American neo-Pentecostal piety is the practice of praying for baptism in the Holy Spirit. This practice together with the experiences which follow from it sets the attitudinal context for regular charismatic prayer gatherings. In praying for Spirit baptism one asks the Spirit of Jesus to transform one just as he transformed the Apostles on the first Pentecost. The prayer presupposes a personal repentance for sin and an acknowledgment that salvation is God's free gift. And it is rooted in the conviction that the saving love of Christ reaches out to "me" personally. The prayer is uttered with the presupposition that the Spirit of Christ is as sovereignly free in dispensing his gifts now as he was on the first Pentecost. It presupposes, therefore, that all the gifts described in the New Testament are available today, if men open their hearts to the Spirit.

In neo-Pentecostal circles all of these beliefs and attitudes are frequently summed up under the ambiguous formula that "Pentecost is an ongoing event in the life of the Church". The formula is ambiguous because it often cloaks over serious discrepancies in the theological interpretation of the meaning of Pentecost.

[5] For the text of the American bishops' statement, see E. O'Connor, *op. cit.*, pp. 291–3.

The most obvious discrepancies exist between those closely associated with denominational Pentecostalism and charismatic Christians who belong to churches with a stronger sacramental tradition.

Among Protestant Pentecostals, to say that Pentecost is an ongoing event in the life of the Church tends to imply that the gift of tongues is the only true test of the arrival of the Pentecostal Spirit in the life of a given individual. It is assumed that each individual is, therefore, called to receive the gift of tongues and cannot truly consider himself as Spirit-baptized until he does.

Such beliefs often represent a fusion of popular Calvinist piety with a fairly fundamentalistic reading of Acts 2. From revivalism, Protestant Pentecostalism tends to derive an unusual preoccupation with the initial conversion experience. And with exegetical naïveté, it generalizes the need for glossolalia to all Christians. This simplistic approach to Spirit-baptism fails to explain, however, why Luke makes no mention of tongues in the case of the three thousand baptized on Pentecost, or why Paul, in 1 Cor. 12. 30, assumes that not all Spirit-baptized people speak in tongues.

Neo-Pentecostals do not subscribe uniformly to such an interpretation of Spirit-baptism. Catholic charismatics have on the whole abandoned the designation "Pentecostal" and prefer instead to speak of the charismatic renewal of the whole Church. They present Spirit-baptism as a prayer for the full release of the graces of the sacraments of initiation, without demanding tongues of all. Catholic charismatics see glossolalia as a genuine gift of the Spirit and tend to expect it to be present in an ordinary prayer group. But they do not regard the gift as mandatory for the Spirit-baptized.[6]

II. Sacramental Implications of Neo-Pentecostal Piety

The prayer experience described in the first part of this essay is theologically neutral on those precise points which tend to

[6] K. McDonnell and A. Bittlinger, *The Baptism in the Holy Spirit as an Ecumenical Problem* (Notre Dame, 1972); K. McDonnell, "Catholic Pentecostalism Problems in Evaluation", *Dialogue* 9 (1970), pp. 34–54; J. Ford, "The Theology of Tongues in Relationship to the Individual", *Bible Today*, 48 (1970), pp. 3,314–20.

divide Catholics and evangelical Protestants. Those issues are largely foundational and sacramental.

The foundational issue is concerned with providing an adequate descriptive interpretation of the Christian faith experience. Protestant Pentecostal piety tends to be coloured by an "inner light" model of the Christian experience. That model tends to dissociate the illumination of the Spirit from a sacramental or hierarchical context. As a consequence it tends to produce subjectivism in worship and an antinomianism in one's relation to church leaders.

The official Catholic stance towards the charismatic dimension of the faith experience is indicated in *Lumen Gentium*, 12. The Catholic position presupposes that in the Pentecostal era, conversion and the gifts of the Spirit are mediated to the individual by the presence of the sacramental community. And the sacramental system grounds the community's hierarchical structure.

The pastoral problem posed by neo-Pentecostalism is, therefore, obvious. Is it possible to reconcile a form of piety that stems from a tradition with individualistic, subjectivistic and antinomian tendencies with a sacramental, hierarchical faith commitment? Clearly if one brings an individualistic, antinomian interpretation to the experience of charismatic prayer, one's piety will develop in an individualistic, antinomian direction. There is, however, a theological approach to the charisms which not only does not oppose charismatic prayer to the sacramental, hierarchical dimension of the Church but which sees them as integrally related.

A charism is a gift of the Spirit. A gift of the Spirit is an enabling call. The call of the Spirit is twofold: to sanctification and to service. The call to sanctification is a call to put on the mind of Christ (Phil. 2. 5), to enter into the relation of adoptive sonship in Jesus' image. The purpose of sacramental baptism cannot, then, be adequately understood apart from the gifts of sanctification.

Growth in the gifts of sanctification matures into service. Christian service is twofold: the service of worship and the service of one's fellow men, both inseparably interrelated. The gifts of service are the Spirit's call to service. The sacrament of confirmation is an ecclesial summons to discern one's gift of service.

For the sacrament presupposes that every believer should grow spiritually to the point at which his life is visibly transformed by the gifts of service as were the Apostles on Pentecost.

Moreover, the charismatic differentiation of the community through the gifts of service helps ground the vocational sacraments of orders and marriage. For these sacraments give visible expression to two kinds of public service within the community.

The sacraments of forgiveness and of the anointing of the sick are, finally, the sacramental ritualization of the Church's early ministry of faith healing. Since the call to the priesthood includes a call to the administration of both of these sacraments, one must conclude that among the "ordinary" "hierarchical" gifts is the gift of healing. Individuals may possess the gift of healing to an extraordinary degree, even if they are not members of the hierarchy; and one may, of course, pray for spiritual and physical healing outside of a sacramental context.[7]

Finally, the Eucharist is the sacrifice of the new covenant, the covenant visibly and charismatically sealed in the hearts of believers on Pentecost. Since the gifts effect the visible transformation of believers, they belong, all of them, to the primordial sacramentality of the Church. In Catholic prayer groups it is not uncommon to celebrate the Eucharist as the culmination of the charismatic prayer gathering. Some allow for a period of spontaneous charismatic prayer after communion. Experience has shown that the theophantic character of charismatic prayer described in the earlier part of this essay enhances the sacramentality of the eucharistic service, while the sacrament fulfils and completes the primordial sacramentality of charismatic prayer.

III. Ecumenical Promise

American neo-Pentecostalism is rich in ecumenical promise. It is providing a shared faith experience for Christians of different communions. But that promise will fade unless communions with a rich sacramental, hierarchical tradition can effectively integrate charismatic and sacramental forms of worship. A sound theological rationale for effecting such an integration exists. But it will come only with adequate theological and pastoral leader-

[7] D. Gelpi, *Pentecostal Piety* (New York, 1972), pp. 3–58.

ship. At present the most serious threat to integration is premature and undirected ecumenical contact among neo-Pentecostals of different communions with a concomitant acceptance of fundamentalistic interpretations of the charismatic experience. As the American Catholic charismatic renewal grows numerically, the burden for supplying intellectual and pastoral leadership will of necessity fall upon the ordained clergy. Whether the American clergy will be able to surmount its rationalism and anti-Protestantism in sufficient numbers to provide the needed leadership, only history will tell.

Enzo Bianchi

Bose: An Interconfessional Community in Italy

NOT SO many years ago Bose was a deserted village, up on the Serra hills, near Magnano in Piedmont, Italy. Today it is the home of a community of Christians of different denominations. Both Catholic and Protestant men and women have settled there in order to put the gospel into practice in celibacy and communal living. The Bose community is not a religious congregation, it does not form part of a parish, it is not an ecumenical sect, and least of all is it a new church. It is a community, developing a monastic ministry and searching for unity among Christians.

I. ORIGINS AND HISTORY

The story of Bose began at Turin in 1963–1965, those early years of *aggiornamento* and awakening of youthful challenge or contestation. While still an undergraduate, I persuaded young Catholics, Waldensians, Evangelical Christians and Baptists to take part, in a house in the Via Piave, in a common endeavour inspired by interconfessional biblical study, prayer and a service of welcome.

Since Piedmont is one of those few parts of Italy where there are many Protestants and Waldensians, the concrete situation and rising tension in the Church provided us with first-hand ecumenical perspectives and prospects.

Catholic members of our community met every evening in order to recite the Hours; we devoted one evening of each week to commemorating the Lord's supper and taking part in fraternal talk. This was one of the earliest spontaneous church groups in Italy; it undoubtedly inspired the formation of other such groups in Piedmont.

As their university days drew to a close, members of the community became aware of their vocations. I decided to find a poor and remote house, as somewhere to live and as a meeting place and point of reference for those now going off on separate ways in response to the calls of life and work. It was then that I came to Bose, near Magnano, on the big moraine ridge running between Biella and Ivrea, a district abandoned by the peasants during the war, and took a house there. Next to the village was a half-ruined Romanesque church. We began to repair it in September 1966 and this was the last occasion that we worked together as a group.

As soon as the church was in a reasonable state of repair, we were able to recite the Hours there. We rented a few houses and restored them too, so as to be able to live in poverty and simplicity. I was alone for a while, but even in those early days I was already visited by people looking for a life of prayer led apart from others. The community really began in the summer of 1968, when I met Daniel Attinger, a young Swiss Reformed pastor and two Catholic girls, all of whom wanted to live in an ecumenical community.

We felt the need to understand and experience more deeply cenobitic monasticism and its historical legacy. Since we could only do this by participating in the life of a monastic community, some of us went off for a while to various Catholic Trappist monasteries, others to Reformed communities, and others to Greek Orthodox communities.

Our first members began their community life on 6 August 1968. A few days later Domenico Ciardi, who was there to make a retreat, asked to stay on. This new vocation came as a sign and confirmation of the path we had chosen. But difficulties had already arisen in the period of working towards community life, and were not lacking in this new period. The church authorities did not understand the interconfessional character of our way of life and feared it.

We were several times asked to leave the diocese and we were forbidden to share the same Eucharist. Then came a stage of serious difficulties between our community and the Catholic hierarchy. We suffered, but persisted, and accepted the difficulties as a sign of growth. More vocations—including a Catholic priest—arrived. We now had twelve members, three of them women. Relations with the churches have altered, many causes of distrust have vanished and today the bishop of Turin acts as guarantor of communion between the local church and the community.

On Easter Sunday morning 1973, the first brethren pronounced their final commitment to the communal life in celibacy, before God and their brothers and sisters, and in the presence of representatives of the Christian churches from which members of the community came and to which they still belong.

All the members of the Bose community are celibate. Since this is a characteristic of cenobitic monasticism, the adjective "monastic" is explicitly used to describe our manner of living. But we are not really concerned with definitions and we look upon ourselves as ordinary Christians who are looking for God and trying to bear witness to Christ by living the gospel. This is always our absolute life rule.

Of course we have a debt to the monastic tradition, for it has handed down the communal way of life and has developed those aspects of the gospel that are particularly relevant to that way of life. We have no hesitation in acknowledging our debt to Basil with regard to our community structure, to Benedict with regard to prayer, and to Francis with regard to our attitude and life style. Yet, for each and every one in the community, our guideline is the gospel, as tested and proved in everyday situations and our life as a whole.

Looking back over the history of the community so far, we can distinguish three stages. The first stage was marked by the coming together of so many people drawn together by a common vocation, a sense of radical commitment and a bond of charity. They left their possessions, homes and families and entered a vocation without security. In the second stage those people became a community. This phase was marked by spiritual growth, comparison with other experiments, and consolidation through our experience of our original insights.

In the third and present period, our members have reached the point where they can make a definite choice in favour of this kind of monastic living along a number of spiritual lines that make up the rule and are agreed to by all. But the community does not look for a legal, artificial recognition by the church authorities and does not intend to ask for the rule to be approved. It is a community of ordinary baptized people who are committed to celibacy and have no other link with the Church than that which other Christians have—the bond of communion!

The community sent out its first new fraternity in the autumn of 1972, when two of the brethren, a Catholic and a Protestant, went to a part of Switzerland which is inhabited by Catholics and Protestants and many Italian immigrants. That new foundation gives service to the churches by means of prayer and pastoral work and carries out social work among the immigrants.

II. Mixed and Interconfessional Communal Life

I will now try to describe some of the elements that distinguish our community life. First of all, it has both men and women in it. Five years of life in common have enabled us to prove that it is possible to live together in this way. We have not failed to take account of fundamental psychological facts, and our guests and the outside world have accepted our way of life as credible. Instead of being ambiguous and arousing all kinds of suspicion, our consecrated celibacy has succeeded in making us brothers and sisters in Christ. Needless to say the relationship between the sexes is one of distance and discretion, maintained so as to keep us free of insurmountable confusion and trouble. But the spirit of fraternity is complete and intact. Our hearts are full of gratitude to one and all for the achievements and mutual solidarity that we have accomplished and lived over these years. We believe that these things can often keep the celibate from even pathological attitudes and states!

Then there is the fact that we belong to differing confessions or denominations. We are Catholics and Protestants who are trying to live together once again after four centuries of separation. At the beginning, this naturally seemed to be evangelical boldness bordering on folly, but today the community's inner life and experience testify to the need for unity. The word of God, the rhythm of our spiritual life together, and acceptance of one community will, have all led us to a faith and a living theology that unite rather than divide us. But it should be borne in mind that the community is neither Catholic nor Protestant—it is a community of Catholics and Protestants, and each member seeks to remain in communion with the Church that brought him to life in Christ.

At the beginning, we ran up against the harsh reality of division continuing among us in spite of many uniting factors. This came to light especially in the Sunday Eucharist, the Catholics celebrating this in the morning, the Protestants in the afternoon. Why should we be divided? Is Christ divided? Visitors found our behaviour in this regard absurd; we ourselves reached a point where we could not understand it any more; yet we did not wish to make intercommunion a spontaneous enthusiastic or emotional gesture or to break with our churches. After two years of theological discussion, we took the decision to put intercommunion into effect, not as a clandestine act, but after giving notice to the proper authorities. This lasted a year, then had to cease in obedience to the Catholic authority. We had in fact specified that for us it was essential to remain in communion with the churches and to be ready to return to distinct separate eucharists if intercommunion was explicitly forbidden.

However, our interconfessional life is making real progress, to the benefit of all denominations. It is demanding faithfulness to the gospel and has taught us that unity of the churches needs to be accompanied by true reform of the churches and victory over confessionalism.

III. COMMUNITY STRUCTURES

The community is quite clear about its intentions for the future. It does not wish to become another order. It does not wish to grow beyond the size that enables well-articulated fraternal living to be carried on, the primary sociological unit being about fifteen to twenty people. It does not wish to have specific tasks. Members only want to live the life of the gospel in a radical way adapted to the modern world. This desire alone is sufficient for admittance to the community. Entry is granted when the request is accepted by the council of the brothers and sisters of Bose. Anyone who wishes to join is asked to leave his possessions behind and to undergo liturgical reception after a period of probation. This is a sign of definite and total commitment to the community. Monastic profession follows after a few years. It is merely an explicit indication to the churches of the decision taken during probation and during the liturgical reception by the community.

The common life is lived according to a daily rhythm marked by periods of work and periods of prayer. Everyone works, so as not to be dependent on anyone, and if possible maintains the profession, trade or work that he had when he entered. Each works among other people, in order that there shall be no paid work done within the community and so as to avoid creating the self-sufficient life that is typical of abbeys. In this way, the community ensures that it can live in poverty without becoming a centre of economic power. Each member's wages are made over to the brother in charge of them, so that everything is shared. Each member receives a sum of money for his needs and requirements during the whole of the month. All do the necessary manual work and share the ministry of hospitality. Specialization is avoided as far as possible, except in professional work. Men and women do the same tasks by turn, in an attempt to overcome the age-old subjection of women to men, which is, of course, also present in religious life.

Besides being based on the communal possession of goods, the community's style of living also follows the precepts of poverty and simplicity. Except for the simple houses providing shelter and living quarters, the community has no property and is not engaged in any economic enterprise. Earnings from wages and salaries (some members are teachers, others manual workers, others office workers) barely cover living and hospitality expenses.

Finally, the community has no head. No one is father, master or director. Decisions are taken in weekly meetings of the council and whoever presides watches over the community's spiritual progress and application of decisions taken and accepted in council. The chairman has no power or authority to make regulations, but there is complete obedience to the council, in the light of the rule, which continues to be our means of fraternal communion and the instrument for gauging one's own degree of participation in the community.

IV. Prayer

In accordance with ancient custom, prayer sets the rhythm of the morning, afternoon and evening, each of which is a three-hour period. Communal prayer consists of an office sung in Italian, and it includes both praise of God and intercession for the brethren.

In order to enable everyone, and not simply initiated members of the community, to pray together, a new form has been devised, taking its inspiration basically from the Roman office, but including liturgical texts from the various Christian churches, all adapted to the spirituality of contemporary man. New prayers have been composed to take account of man's contemporary problems in his dialogue with God. A choral rhythmical translation of the Psalms has been made from the original texts, which can be easily understood by ordinary people—peasants, manual workers and intellectuals. In this way, prayer is praise and listening for the word. It is not a flight from the world, or an alibi, but deeply something that is an integral part of life and praxis. Working out this new liturgy that takes account of the churches' traditions has been one of the community's major undertakings.

V. Hospitality

We think that our celibacy enables us to be hospitable in a very intensive way. Hospitality is a most necessary ministry, since it is a fundamental reaction against the isolation suffered by modern man in depersonalized cities and against lack of encounter and dialogue between the generations. In 1972 more than five thousand persons came to us in this way. What were they looking for?

Some came looking for a praying community that would help them in prayer. They wanted to see us as "monks", assuring the Church of continuous prayer. Others came to learn about our community life—how it is arranged, how our interpersonal relationships function in practice. Others again were interested in ecumenism, and wanted to learn how it was possible for Catholics and Protestants to live together after four centuries of being separated. Others came in order to be quiet, to keep silence, becase they were in a crisis, or were discouraged. Finally—we say this not too loudly and with great humility—there are those that came here to live Christian and sacramental lives because they can no longer do so in the official Church. We try to give a reply to all these various needs, which are not mutually contradictory. We often do not feel that we are living up to that clear vision and sign that our community has rapidly come to be. We are helped by strict poverty in our environment and by the fact that we remain small—in our actions, our means and as an institution.

During the whole period of contestation we did not become exultant. We tried to remain faithful to our everyday life, life made up of little things, manual work, the affairs of ordinary people living in common as a family, to professional work in the world, to our daily search to bear witness to the Christian faith. Our contestation has always been one of patience, avoidance of publicity and rejection of intolerance and fanaticism, but it has also been a life of radical commitment and liberty.

VI. Commitment in the Church and in the World

The community is carrying on a typically church work, preaching, holding Bible courses and meetings between Catholics and Protestants and co-ordinating spontaneous ecclesial groups.

Finally, our service to the churches finds expression in that common life that is known as monastic life. Celibacy is lived in interior certainty of a calling from God and in readiness to be open to and to serve each other. It is also expression of our waiting for Christ's coming.

In a word, the community wishes to respond actively to the need for renewal in religious life and it tries to play a prophetic role in the contemporary world. Commitment to the world is not a choice, even less an effort, for the Bose community. Members work like all other men and women, committing themselves together with them to the social reality where work takes them, in co-responsibility, solidarity and struggle together with others at stress points where justice is being sought, without fear of dirtying one's hands. All the members of the community have the duty to join in and be responsive to the demands of justice. It is for them as individuals to choose their own political or social sphere of action, to give it content and make that content visible. Belonging to the monastic tradition cannot excuse us from fighting for the emancipation of man wherever we are called to be present in a special way. It is therefore necessary to make an effort of the imagination in order to bring the believer's authentic identity to that task of emancipation that all other men and women are engaged in. Flight from the world must never be an alibi or a refusal of responsibility—it should always be a challenge, a contestation of the world's methods, which are under the law of power, money and success. In the community, our various experiences are compared and judged, but on no other criterion than that of obedience to the gospel and the calls of justice.

VII. Conclusion

In the work of building up a community, effort has in the past been directed to giving a sign that might ensure historical continuity for an original insight. We prefer our community to be a sign for today, that is, a sign for our generation that has no need for continuity. Continuity has indeed often led to massive institutionalism and to sclerosis, so our community is a provisional one, a temporary one in the sense that it commits us only in a definite way, and we are but few. Our experience can also be shared by young people who may wish to commit themselves to the monastic life for a time, as a preparation for marriage or life in society. It tries to be a normal sign, based on an inner call from God and a gratuitous, evangelical choice. For us, what is important is living the gospel and we live it in celibacy and in community.

Translated by Firmin O'Sullivan

John-David Robinson

"Word out of Silence" Symposium[1]

THE symposium on spiritualities in world religions held in August 1972 at Mount Saviour Monastery in the serene hills of upper New York State, U.S.A., should perhaps be called a *celebration* of some major world spiritualities. This contemplative conference, which was characterized by both celebration and dialectical colloquia, provided insights into a "one-world spirituality" emerging in our time from the convergence of many historic traditions. And it was itself an event in this evolution. We were not gathered only to celebrate the past but to create the future, as Thomas Berry, professor of history of religions at Fordham University, reminded the assembly.

The classic sense of symposium as a party of friends sharing free-flowing "sacramental" and mythic poetry and prose has largely given way to an academic conference of scholars presenting and arguing theses. Our gathering of spiritual pilgrims was a convocation to share contemplation of the cosmic and human dance of the Word. Faithful to the more ancient sense, our symposium was a drinking-party in the Spirit. The week-long banquet of Jewish, Christian, Sufi, Hindu and Buddhist liturgies, meditation disciplines and discourses was shared by one hundred and fifty carefully selected university professors, superiors of sisterhoods, Catholic and Protestant college community ministers, spiritual formation directors of religious congregations, monks

[1] The complete symposium proceedings will appear in an illustrated volume, "Word Out of Silence", available from Mount Saviour Monastery, Pine City, New York, 14871, U.S.A.

and friars of several communities, and young people from a variety of traditional and experimental learning communities, with noted spiritual masters from many parts of the world. These participants were invited to constitute together a true arcadian academy within the pastoral setting of the monastery. They had been chosen from diverse backgrounds and levels of understanding: Socrates with the Slave Boy was our learning model. Christian scholars met with gnostic magi, faithful Catholic teaching sisters encountered wise men from the East who are the charismatic leaders of the American "counter-culture", and uncommitted young people on wide-ranging intense interior pilgrimages and priests responsible for confessing, reforming and passing on Christian tradition together sought techniques for opening the third eye of the heart.

In preparing this contemplative convocation in the Word the director had two "words" of St Ignatius of Antioch in his heart; "God is one, and has revealed himself in Jesus Christ his Son, who is his Word, proceeding from Silence, who in all that he was and did gladdened the heart of the One who sent him" (*Magn*. 8). The fullness beyond all being is the divine simplicity, God's Silence: the Father is related to the Son as Silence to Word. And, "if any of you has God within himself, let that man understand my longings and feel for me ... (for) ... there is living water within me which speaks and says within me, 'Come to the Father'" (*Rom*. 6, 7). The living water flowing from and back to the absolute source has been speaking in our common human being in many dry places in the technological desert of our time. Moreover, the intercultural *kairos* is pregnant to produce a global spirituality. Quite simply it was the living water of the Spirit urging the symposium in the director and others who had heard its murmur in their hearts' deepest desires. It was the river of the Spirit moving through history which gathered us together in diversity and in unity in the Word proceeding from that full Silence, simplicity of the Absolute, which is at once our source and our goal. We came together to explore a common world of non-verbal communication and to create a new cultural world of common discourse as we sought the mystery of the centre in which our separate world-views converge.

The symposium was conceived as a dynamic icon of this contemplative centre, the absolute fullness which is the *premise* rather than the goal of interreligious dialectic. The mystery of the Absolute has been communicated to individuals and so to traditions in the past: our present purpose was to celebrate that Source together and *then* to examine categories of description and explore the fashioning of a common language of experience. The dialectic of encounter between religions is commonly the exact reverse of our conviction. This alone makes our symposium significant.

Personal experience is the key to salvation in our time. This is clearly manifested in our American society in widespread sensitivity-training centres and encounter-technique groups, in communes of young people seeking basic values, and in meditation and pentecostal movements in middle-class middle-aged "Middle America". In our symposium we sought individually and together experience of the divine in Nature; in our marvellously varied human nature—with its celebratory words, rites and meditation *ways*; and in God's Silence beyond the dance of all being in the Word. Throughout we sought that divine simplicity experienced as interior silence into which we are introduced by traditional wisdom in our religions.

The days followed the basic time-table of the host community of Benedictine monks, with symposium events integrated into their distinctive life. Participants rose from the little death each night to meditate for an hour before dawn in one of several ways: traditional Western monastic Vigil service of psalmody and hymnody followed by *Lectio Divina*: *zazen*, Zen sitting meditation, a practice in still the discursive intellect; the physical-spiritual integration of Hatha-Yoga; Sufi meditation and dancing; Tai Chi Chuan the Chinese eurhythmics; Greek Orthodox hesychast meditation with the Jesus Prayer.

At dawn each day all gathered to silently greet the new day as the great crimson sun rose in the mist over the gentle farmlands; all together then entered the chapel for a common Morning Service in one of the traditions. Pir Vilayat Inayat Khan, head of the Sufi Order in the West, presided at a sunrise service of prayers from many mystical traditions; Alan Watts, Taoist *shaman* and Anglican Christian priest, led a mantric service of worship *sabda*, pure sound, another morning; and Raimundo

Panikkar, Hindu and Catholic Christian, scholar and priest of
the Word, celebrated a great Cosmic Christian Liturgy from
within the womb of the night to the bright dawn of the final
day of the symposium.

Mornings were devoted to the Word proper with discourses by
distinguished participants. Following each talk there was an hour
of silence for reflection before responses. Thus an attempt was
made to immerse the participants in a matrix of silence from
which words could assume real power—an attempt more or less
successful since most participants were accustomed to the conferences of "Babel" and found it difficult to enter the marvellous
paradisiacal garden of Silence where words are precious beyond
commercial purchase. Opening and concluding all conferences
with silent prayer and chanting of prayers, *sutras* and invocations
in a different tradition each time helped establish the equanimity
of an integral meditative atmosphere.

Professor Panikkar, of Benares, India and Santa Barbara, California, brilliantly directed the theme of the gathering to a further
contemplative depth in his address, "The Silence of the Word:
Non-Dualistic Polarities". Using revelation texts from the Hindu
scriptures he disclosed the Word as the incarnation of the primal
Silence itself: the Son is the *Being* of the Father. As one young
man put it, Panikkar's talk gave him a "jnāna high"—and many
listeners experienced in it an ecstasy of the *intellectus*, a marvellous *perichoresis* of the divine Persons dancing together before
the ages of the world in their minds and hearts.

Joshu Sasaki Roshi, Zen master who had been priest of the
mountain temple in Japan where the famous Hakuin received
enlightenment, reminded us again and again that although ob-
jectifying is a necessity of our human nature we should seek
periods of the pure experience of being beyond the subject-object
dichotomy. Pure experience of being is available precisely within
our usual condition for those who will open the inner-eye of
pure consciousness. This, in a single Zen barque of recognition,
is what life is essentially all about. Christians could call this the
realization of the presence of the kingdom of heaven within
themselves now. We Christians who tend to drift and coast along
our divinely given short-cut into the heart of God by reason of
our adoption as sons in the Only-Begotten Son, need to be awak-

ened in shame from our sloth by the holy pagans outside the artificially cosy family household of the Faith. The ruthless honesty, profundity and earnest gravity of spiritual practice among those we Christians hold have no such family claims as we on God as Father, shows our faint-hearted filial position to be sad where it is not presumptive. Jesus the Surprising One may have many surprises in store for us smug younger brothers! We Christians, relying too completely on the initiative which is unquestionably God's in the illumination and transformation of our human nature, have neglected to explore and refine practices of spiritual anthropology as far as we should in preparation for the higher gifts and in response to the grace that is in us. We have much to learn in understanding our human nature from Eastern wisdom traditions which possess many more centuries of carefully elaborated reflection on spiritual experience than we. Now seems the providential time in the history of the Church to humbly learn from "the others" whom the Spirit has meanwhile not left orphans.

Swami Venkatesananda, a phenomenally happy, lightsome *guru* who is on teaching pilgrimage around the world much of every year from his anchorage on the island of Mauritius in the Indian Ocean, beautifully demythologized the *guru* from a usual place of idolized hero. His conference concerned our human being as *ahimsa*, perfect integration, peacefulness beyond polarities. He urged the participants to realize themselves as manifestations of the divine Light, the true Guru. His teaching was particularly pertinent for all those engaged in political protest and working for social change. We need to clarify our personal being if we would bring reconciliation and peace to others. Swami Venkatesananda's conference struck the present writer as pure Gautama Buddhist reform within the Brahmanic master-disciple tradition, similar in scope to Jesus' reform within Pharisaic Judaism.

Archimandrite Kallistos Ware, university lecturer in Eastern Orthodox Christianity at Oxford, gave a serenely powerful presentation of the tradition of spiritual authority in the Orthodox churches. The authority of the *geron* or *staretz* is one given directly by the Holy Spirit. The way into which such a spiritual father leads others is into *being* prayer rather than simply making prayers. Emphasized was the solitary history of many spiritual fathers, which issues in universal compassion and intercession. A *staretz* remains responsible and faithful to his spiritual children beyond the grave. Coming from his monastery of St John the Theologian on the island of Patmos, Greece, Father Kallistos reminded his fellow pilgrims at the symposium that a true theologian is a person in whom God and his Word are constantly prayerfully present, rather than a scholar who is simply learned in theology. His own scholarly service to our convocation was infused with the deep, quiet contemplative conviction of the Hesychast tradition. Listening to him and participating in his Vigils in the Jesus Prayer one thought of the clarity and joy of the true gnosis in Clement of Alexandria's radiant hymn to Christ the Pedagogue.

A leader of the American consciousness-expansion explosion with the L.S.D. drug in the nineteen-fifties and sixties, Richard Alpert, formerly at Harvard, has gone on to explore non-chemical spiritual disciplines in India as a dedicated yogi. Now named Ram Dass by his guru in the Himalayas, and entitled Baba (little grandfather) by his followers, he is a key figure in the counterculture search for personal integration and transcendence. His talk on experiences and insights in reconciling polarities in himself gave profound observations into the causes of evil in our society. Personal integration achieved through meditation is of practical use in solving the problems of our increasingly polarized, fragmented, destructive society. Hippies beget cops, the disease of consuming possessiveness begets theft, self-justification injustice: Baba Ram Dass is a contemporary St Francis. Very many rejoice in the pointers towards peace he is able to give from his own spiritual pilgrimage.

A "New Age" of radical consciousness expansion through esoteric techniques has dawned in our day among young people disenchanted in the neon-night of a power and material success oriented society. The new mystic seekers are the children of the affluent society. Having found their parent morally bankrupt they are now in search of *personal experience* of the ultimate ground for values, including those of religion and morality. The ancient gnostic wisdom of the Sufis attracts increasing numbers of young people. They are attuned to its cosmic consciousness and sensitivity to all living beings in contrast to our ecological depravities. And the Sufi doctrine of a divine alchemy in the human individual in contact with the transcendent Source is a catalyst for many whose consciousness has been awakened from slumber by chemical "trips". Pir Vilayat Inayat Khan, Sorbonne and Oxford educated successor to his Indian father as head of the Sufi Order in the West, spoke at the symposium about the *seed* of individual being which we must seek beyond the phenomena of personal growth in order to be in touch with the divine ground of our beings. And the Sufi tradition of *dhikrs*, mantrams of human sound evoking the primeval music of the spheres, vocal tones reverberating the cosmic mysteries of the divine Word, fascinated many Christians as Pir Vilayat introduced the assembly to this esoteric ontology.

Father Francis Martin, a Scripture scholar of Madonna House Community in Canada and at present a core member of the charismatic community in Rome, witnessed to the scandal of the historical Jesus as the cause of our infinitude. Defeat by death, radical human limitation, a political rabble-rouser's crucifixion—an unlikely candidate to be cause of our infinitely expanded personal being. Glorified consciousness *now* and beyond death? Jesus Risen? What does He mean in the Spirit for us now? Human limitation as the occasion for divine infinitude is a supreme paradox difficult for most "spiritual people" to stomach. Yet the enduring humanity of Christian mysticism is the narrow gate into the supercosmic garden of paradise for us. Paradise is not to be recovered or projected but realized in ourselves now by *caritas* for one another. Divine infinitude is most clearly grasped as limitless love, *agape*: the goal of transcendental consciousness is boundless participation in and infinite manifestation of that divine being to one another.

Alan Watts, one of the first visionaries among us, has for three decades been working towards a Taoist spirituality of aseity and unicity within polarized Christianity. His discourse "Unity in Contemplation", which concluded our symposium, was an exposition of that trans-cultural consciousness essential for solving many of our chief church problems at present. Our symposium was in many respects a logical offspring of his life work, and the director here wishes to acknowledge Watts' oblique influence in his own history.

The mystery of evil erupted among us in incidents involving cultural privilege and lack of privilege as well as subtle racism veiled by liberal sentimentality. Racism is the tragic wound in the body politic of the United States, and any serious event in the Spirit here is sure to be pained by it. The polarities producing evil in our human being were explored by spokesmen from several religious traditions.

Nature's mysteries being perhaps less complex than those of our human nature, and in any case morally neutral, the natural shape of the day was emphasized at the symposium. Yet one was aware that all nature is in travail awaiting the final redemption and transfiguration of the *whole body* of the Word, and we Christian humans are the seeds of cosmic apotheosis. The sun's meridian at noon was a natural high point to break off the words of dialectic for silent worship in the Word, followed by the gathering of small groups for *satsang*, informal serious conversation with masters during luncheon. Sunset and the descent into the daily tomb of night was celebrated with a Vesper Service either in the chapel or on a hill-top. Swami Satchidananda, founder of Integral Yoga Institutes around the world, led the assembly in chanting the mystical primal word *OM*, with evening *ragas*, and offered a *puja* of fire, flowers and fruits to the Absolute revealed in every form and approached along every spiritual way, although dwelling in inaccessible light. The awe of his offering could be well marked by Christians who often tend to a terrible cosiness with God because of the gift of our Christianing in divinity through Jesus. Archimandrite Kallistos celebrated Byzantine Vespers. One evening we danced gravely in the Word as Sasaki Roshi led us in Zen *kinhin*, formal walking meditation with chant, using our powerful Christian acclamation-invocation *Kyrie eleison* intoned from the deep Japanese *hara*, rather than a Buddhist sutra. Another evening we ecstatically danced far into the night lighted by the mystic fires burning in Hasidic tales sung by Rabbi Shlomo Carlebach, well known to the "holy beggars" in many parts of the world for whom he breaks the bread of the one Word.

Perhaps half of the participants were Roman Catholics. Many

said they experienced the symposium as a unique occasion of their Christian Faith seeking understanding. Illumination came in our celebrations where several traditions were gathered together in the Name of the One who is always surprising, always breaking out of our structures and our expectations with the New Creation. And many Christians got lightening glimpses in Eastern meditation techniques as to *how* they might further act on the gospel counsel to shut the private door of the heart to pray to our Father who hears us in secret. Many participants said that as a result of the symposium experience in words and in rites they are compelled to reform their own spiritual practice to plumb their own deepest desires more fully, and to cast the line of their hope truly into the heart of God.

Throughout the masters proved themselves worthy of their titles by constant selfless service to the other participants. It was clear in widely differing religious traditions that there is only one divine Master, and those who among us are called masters are in fact our distinguished servants. With such servants it was quite a party in the Spirit!

Segundo Galilea

Spiritual Awakening and Movements of Liberation in Latin America

THE first question that we have to ask in this context is whether it is possible or realistic to talk of spiritual awakening among the militant Christians of Latin America.

At a first glance, and taking the term in the sense in which it has been traditionally understood in this continent, the situation would seem to be the reverse. Judging from what has happened in the seminaries and apostolic movements in the past ten or fifteen years, the spirituality of the élite in Latin America would seem to have fallen into decay. Discovering the "religious" value of the profane and of temporal action, they have moved away in the practical application of their faith from any attitude that could lead to dualism or evasion. This has produced a crisis in traditional spirituality—many traditional practices have disappeared, to be replaced by a search for more secularized and committed forms of expression.

This crisis came about because of the difficulty in finding valid forms for these new expressions of faith. Practices that had become anachronistic were abandoned, sometimes with undue haste, and little new was found to put in their place. This is a normal stage in the evolution of Christians who value commitment more than pious practices. The danger is that without means of expression, their faith will atrophy, and that the secularization of spirituality will become an alibi for spiritual anaemia. This has in fact happened in the case of too many militants over the past few years—they have simply drifted away from the sacramental system of the Church. The crisis of traditional spirituality has meant a considerable decline in attendance at the sacraments.

I. The Causes of the Crisis

The causes of the crisis would seem not to lie only, or even mainly, in the quality of faith of committed Christians. In my view, it arose because their faith was suddenly brought face to face with a new social and cultural situation. This is the challenge that the present generation of Latin-American Christians has to face. Social change for them is a fact, and they are becoming more and more deeply involved in it. Although they may approach it from different ideological standpoints. revolution, as a profound and qualitative change in the unjust society in which they live, has become part of their lives and implies the making of decisions. All too often, they cannot reconcile this with the sort of Christian education they received, based as this was on an ecstatic, devotional, a-historical concept of Christ and the faith, a religion that stressed the other-worldliness of its message, consisted of pious practices and was firmly tied to the existing social system. With the radical change that has taken place in the socio-cultural climate of Latin America and the appearance of revolutionary tendencies, this sort of religion has entered a period of crisis. The traditional faith does not fit into this situation and so has been, as it were, expropriated, having no answers to the new challenges.

These Christians, furthermore, are not passive participants in these changes. They have committed themselves deeply to them, particularly through political channels. For them, the building of a more just society is the indispensable concomitant of the economic, cultural and social liberation for the masses of the workers, peasants and alienated poor of Latin America. The commitment to liberation and the movements it gives rise to take the form of a political commitment.

These commitments—often revolutionary—to the liberation of the oppressed and the political involvement of militant Christians they have produced (even among considerable sections of the clergy) have increased the challenge to traditional theology and spirituality, which found themselves in alien territory. The "political theology" that emerged in Europe failed to interpret their commitment to liberation, until a Latin-American branch of it recently appeared in an attempt to produce a theology of liberation. This has not yet had much influence in the realm of spirituality. Our christology in particular has been lacking in this respect, failing to offer a model and a way to inspire and guide our commitment to liberation. Traditional teaching has presented Christ instead as standing apart from the temporal and political questions of his day, bearing a message simply of personal salvation.

All this has meant that committed Christians have lost sight of the meaning of the sacraments, the liturgy and prayer in general, which they have instinctively come to mistrust as activities alien to the historical development of their continent. There was a crisis of synthesis between political militancy and any form of contemplation, between commitment to liberation and the Word of God.

Finally, I believe that one of the main causes for the decline of religion has been the encounter between many of the new Christians, often organized in left-wing groups or movements, and Marxism. In some cases this has made them question their faith, sometimes purifying it and sometimes making it waver. In others, some of these groups have fallen foul of the hierarchy or of other important sectors of the clergy, and this has led to a cooling of their relations with the Church and a lessening of their participation in its sacramental and spiritual life. These Christians have alienated themselves—or been alienated—in their life of faith.

II. The Reality of an Awakening

Despite the decline and the crisis, I believe that there really is a spiritual awakening, precisely among those Christians who have committed themselves to the cause of liberation. Of late, there have been solid and widespread indications that many of them are rediscovering the meaning of faith and of prayer and doing so through their very commitment. The "contemplative" is beginning to rediscover his place among the "militants".

There are significant pointers to this fact in many quarters. Among those priests who are particularly conscious of the process of liberation, and pastorally committed to it, there is a return to spiritual retreats in the strict sense, with times set aside for silence and prayer. My personal experience, gained from travelling through the various countries of Latin America, is that desire for serious experiences of faith and prayer is just as strong among the young, independently minded clergy and this is equally true where the clergy are found among the more "politicized" sectors of the community, as in the southern tip of the continent. On various retreats that I have given there, the young clergy have insisted particularly on times for adoration and silence. "We have many days of heavy pastoral work, and if we are to work out the strategy of our social commitment we need the moments when we meet to cultivate our spirituality to be not just another day, but a truly contemplative experience."

At the Latin-American Pastoral Institute, where I normally work, the same process has been markedly on the increase during the last two years. Each term, a large number of priests and religious come there from practically every country in the continent. They are a representative selection, and pastorally and socially very "aware", most of them committed in one way or another to the liberation of their people through their apostolic work. I notice that the pastoral course is becoming increasingly imbued with spirituality—there are discussion groups, seminars, periodic retreats, prayer groups. For a considerable number of those taking part, their "recharging" takes place in these moments of deepening their faith, recovering their balance in prayer and so starting on a process of personal conversion.

What is most interesting is that this spiritual awakening is occurring as an ecclesial event in the experience of many committed Christians and groups of Christians. There is an evolution towards a rediscovery of the meaning of the liturgy and of prayer. I have asked several of them, very involved in the socio-political struggle, to comment on what they understand by this awakening, and the consensus of their views is that their commitment to liberation came about at the same time as their commitment to Christianity, though they see various political alternatives for bringing it about. Even though their religious education did not prepare them for it, they still see a strong connection between their politics and their faith.

"All that is contemplative in Christian life is necessary to me to keep alive the ideals that should inspire my liberating practice", said one. "And I have become conscious of this through my commitment to liberation itself."

"The danger in the social struggle and the work of liberation is that others come to be seen as the enemy. One can quickly reach this point unless one clings to Christian values", said another. "This is why the believer must have an infusion of the transcendent, of the gospel, in his life. This he gets through prayer. Otherwise one is in danger of becoming a pragmatist without standards, a slave to sheer political effectiveness, in the Leninist manner. ..."

"Prayer", states another, "and spirituality in general are far from being a brake on my commitment to revolution. On the contrary, they help me to humanize it, to christianize the tactics. ..."

"In the process of liberation, prayer is what marks us out as Christians. It avoids the dualism between faith and practical liberation that led many of our companions to give up the practice of their Christianity. The word of God, the liturgy and true contemplation form the bridge between our commitment to liberation and our convictions as believers. ..."

"In the midst of our involvement, we need to experience the Kingdom and hope. We should not be discouraged and we need the example of dedication that goes beyond immediate experience, which is often disheartening. A serious spirituality assures us of this type of experience. ..."

"The Christian who takes part in movements of liberation will become a contemplative in the measure that he understands God's plan for his brothers and makes this understanding the main inspiration for his commitment. This spirit makes him capable of a universal love, without abandoning his preference for the oppressed ... capable of developing forms of love that are non-party, and certainly non-sectarian, and solidly effective among the poor. ..."

III. Towards a Spirituality of Liberation?

It is not easy to describe the awakening of spirituality that has been stimulated by movements of liberation in Latin America.

Its tendencies are still diffuse, and its direction spontaneous rather than thought out. But these Christians are living by evangelical values found in the same form all over the continent—in Chile, Mexico and the sierras of the Andes, the same formulation of faith in relation to liberation can be found. This allows us to outline the main points of a spirtuality of liberation which has still not found an adequate theological formulation and is lived spontaneously by most of its adherents in a very unstructured form, often with little reference to the liturgy or to the prevailing official spirituality. In this sense it has some similarity with the popular Catholicism of Latin America. I shall try to describe it as it is, rather than as the theologians might like it to be. I shall not attempt to produce a theological formulation of what a spirituality of liberation for Latin America might be, but to document the characteristics of the spiritual awakening that is actually taking place.

1. There is a strong emphasis on "commitment" to the Lord closely linked to giving oneself to one's oppressed brother. Jesus is seen to be present above all in the poor, so that contemplative experience does not come only from different forms of prayer, but from service of liberation performed for the Christ who lives in "the least of the brethren" (Mt. 25. 41). The whole of this pericope from Matthew has been "Latin-Americanized" and these Christians see the "least of their brethren" in all those in Latin America who are suffering from some form of social oppression. So, service of Christ is identified with service of the oppressed.

2. From this standpoint, the sacraments and various forms of prayer become a sort of moment of synthesis between meeting the personal Christ and meeting Christ in "the least of the brethren". These are the moments for refreshing the specifically evangelical content of the commitment to the liberation of these "least of the brethren".

3. One of the convictions most deeply held by these Christians is that there is only one history—in other words, that the history of salvation is one with present historical events in Latin America. In both, liberation plays a major part and salvation, which takes place in history, is for them tied up with the liberation of the

oppressed. They feel themselves to be collaborating with the redeeming Christ in their work for liberation, and so see themselves in the mainstream of the history of salvation. They feel that as they are working for justice to be done to the various categories of poor they are united to God's plan and his saving will. In their minds, salvation and liberation are inextricably linked.

4. For these Christians therefore the choice of liberation coincides with the building up of the Kingdom of God, a kingdom of brotherhood and equality. They see all the work they put into the task of liberation as a contribution to building up a society in which these values will prevail. They are conscious of the need for conversion to the Kingdom and of the work needed to bring this conversion about. This in turn becomes the praxis through which society will be changed into an image and anticipation of this Kingdom. So they look for a way of life that will put this brotherhood and equality into effect, while at the same time providing a prophetic criticism of the prevailing system. Hence the emergence of a communal way of life, of "brotherhoods" or grass-roots communities in which they can be fully committed to the poor and their aspirations and the demands of their faith put into effect.

5. The praxis of liberation, understood as the process by which society is transformed to the benefit of those who suffer oppression, is the historical and privileged form of the exercise of Christian charity. These Christians are very conscious of the fact that love must be effective and historical and for them the effectiveness of love today is measured by its contribution to the process of liberation. Since political activity is the principal means of achieving this liberation—at least at this juncture of history in Latin America—political commitment becomes an expression of Christian charity. Charity becomes political, and politics become a spiritual experience.

In this context, the Christians we are discussing rediscover the evangelical content of the sufferings caused by the commitment to liberation. They identify the persecuted, the deported and the imprisoned with Christ. Extreme situations, such as violence and guerrilla activities, they see as extreme forms of charity—in so far as they are inspired by love of one's oppressed neighbour. And the final expression of this love is to lay down one's life for one's neighbour.

6. These Christians are carrying on a contemporary Latin-American tradition of sensitivity to the problem of poverty. In a continent of poor people, where poverty is caused by the injustice of the system, Christians have been looking for a spirituality of poverty in the form of solidarity with the poor and sharing their lot. Religious, both men and women, have been looking for a life-style embracing extremes of external poverty. The Church of the poor has been understood as a Church that must itself be poor and present among the poorest.

Christians belonging to the groups involved in the struggle for liberation have accepted this basic understanding, but have called passive ways of being present among the poor into question. For them it is not enough to be "like" the poor or to identify them-selves with them. This is not how they understand the "Church of the poor". A strong dose of protest and liberation has to be added to solidarity with the poor and the practice of personal poverty. There has to be a purpose in their sharing the fate of the poor. They have to accompany them on their road to liberation and advancement. Their poverty has to be a commitment to the poor, and they want to see a poor Church not merely lowering itself to share the lot of the exploited classes, but committing itself to join them in their fight for justice.

7. Finally, the last characteristic of the growing spirituality of liberation is that it must contain an element of risk and breaking away. Christians must break away from capitalism and the con-sumer society, and they must accept the risks that accompany such a break-away. This approach is based not only on the Christian themes already noted, such as poverty and the search for a brotherly way of life. It goes further back into biblical history for its sources, to the themes of the Exodus and the wandering in the desert (both, of course, themes long familiar to Christian spiritu-ality).

The Exodus prompts these Christians to a dynamic spirituality, breaking away from the pseudo-Christian images of God and the pseudo-spiritualities produced by bourgeois capitalism in con-formity with the system. The break-away from these along the

lines of the Exodus leads them to a creative spirituality that stimulates them in the fight for liberation and social change. In the
Exodus, they find the biblical basis for the dialectics of liberation
from slavery that is for them the key to the contemporary Latin-
American situation.

The wandering in the desert is part of the same theme. The
break with an unjust system to build a more brotherly form
of society—liberation—requires long periods of sacrifice, austerity
and struggle. There is also a temptation to return to the security
of some aspects of the system and to halt the process of change.
Liberation will have its setbacks and its times of darkness. Many
of these Christians, particularly among the intellectual élite,
equate these times with the Israelites' and Jesus' experience of the
desert. The desert is the place of temptation and the struggle
against the seductions of the world. It is the place of the dark
night of liberation, a place of sacrifice, and of dynamism too. The
Israelites experienced their forty years' wandering in the desert
in quest of the Promised Land, and Jesus was tempted for forty
days in the wilderness. These biblical passages are now re-read
as signposts on the road of the socio-political way of liberation.

Such appear to me to be the principal characteristics of the
spiritual awakening of the movements of liberation.

This is not the time to attempt to evaluate them. They are still
in a spontaneous and fragmentary state and are still obviously
subject to vacillations. Above all, South American Christians are
tempted to turn their socio-political options into a sort of Christian mysticism, or to make an ideology out of spiritual theology.
The most aware of the clergy and laity who belong to these movements are conscious of these dangers.

Because of these dangers, it is vital that theologians collaborate
with these movements, that there should be a permanent contact
between theology and militancy. So, as living Christian experience is brought together with the Word, a more consistent
spiritualiity of liberation will emerge, with its theological and
spiritual components distinguishable, and a clearly Christian
motivation for its commitment to the poor. Taking any sort of
motivation in this direction as theology or spirituality has confused the Christian situation in Latin America at the moment,

and there are some theologies of liberation that are in fact nothing of the sort.

Perhaps it would be appropriate to add in conclusion that the re-awakening of spirituality in Latin America is not confined exclusively to the movements of liberation. There are other important signs of the action of the Spirit visible, such as the Catholic-Pentecostal style prayer groups, the rich spiritual process of the creation of grass-roots communities, the emergence of new forms of religious life, missionary endeavours in the indigenous sub-cultures, and so on. All these movements are not destined to pull in different directions, but to come together and enrich each other, and one of the most significant of them at the present time is clearly the spirituality of liberation.

Translated by Paul Burns

Pierre Raffin

Spiritual Revival and Renewal in the Religious Life

THE five criteria for renewal put before religious institutes by the Decree *Perfectae Caritatis* on the Renewal of the Religious Life are by now familiar: (1) the following of Christ; (2) fidelity to the spirit of the founder; (3) total commitment to the life of the Church; (4) adequate awareness of the conditions of people's lives and of the needs of the Church; (5) desire for genuine spiritual renewal as the motivating force behind all this.

Now, after a number of years of sincere and courageous attempts at *aggiornamento* on the part of religious congregations, one is so often left with the impression that the reforms prescribed by chapters of every kind have been neither sufficiently well-informed nor dependent on the kind of renewal envisaged by *Perfectae Caritatis*; hence the feeling of discouragement and weariness, not to say of failure, which is the present experience of a fair number of religious who have, none the less, co-operated loyally with the renewal programme of Vatican II. To what extent, then, can we regain inspiration sufficiently powerful to rally the forces of religious life and make it credible and attractive once more to active Christians?—that is the question religious institutes should be asking themselves. In fact, as we shall see at the end, it is a question, no more and no less, of rediscovering, as the principle of religious life, as authentic theology of the Holy Spirit, a theology which one cannot elaborate by simply scrutinizing religious institutes from within, but rather by attempting to comprehend the life of the entire ecclesial community. Who, today, would deny that the people of God is well and truly impelled by the Spirit? Signs of what some do not hesitate to call the return of the Spirit can be seen everywhere, and should we doubt it, books and periodicals persist in bringing them all to our notice, from the most modest to the most spectacular. But how far is religious life affected by this spiritual renewal in the Christian community?

I. Spiritual Awakenings lead to a Renewal of Religious Life

This is the first observation we are led to make. More or less everywhere today, Christians are regaining a sense of community and of their responsibilities in the Church, as well as of prayer and the sacramental life. It is particularly striking that many such Christians, in striving to fulfil to the utmost the demands faith makes on them, are rediscovering for themselves the very values traditionally lived by religious.

The Focolare movement,[1] born in Italy thirty years ago, seems especially significant in this connection. It is a lay-inspired movement which aims to combine prayer, meditation, total involvement in the world, and community life, and to bear witness to unity both within the Church and in the ecumenical field. At first, a number of militant young Catholic women belonging to Catholic Action groups, most of them students, decided to live "an authentic Christian life" in a small, loose community (*focolare* means "hearth" in Italian) and very soon other Christians—men and women, celibate or married, lay or religious—were attracted by their project and set up new centres. From amongst these, some very quickly felt compelled to enrol for life in either the male or female branch of the movement and live in community, making vows of poverty, chastity and obedience, but claiming that they remained Christians like any other. The result is that the movement is formed in a series of concentric circles: "focolarini" properly so-called, who have made the three vows; married couples who have dedicated their lives to the movement; and Christians, who without committing themselves to the movement in any formal way live according to its spiritual inspiration and share in the life of its communities.

[1] M.-F. d'Autun, "L'Idéal des Focolarini", in *Informations Catholiques Internationales*, 380 (1971), p. 3.

Having followed the lay section of the Dominican Order as it carried out its own researches we have come to know several lay people who have travelled along a similar path. Attracted by the charism of the founder of the Order of Preachers, they endeavour to find a place for its evangelical inspiration in the context of their family or professional lives, and some have even gone on to make of their lay commitment in the Dominican family a true profession, involving vows and some share in the life of the community.[2] Obviously we are too well aware of the aberrations of the old third orders, which in many cases were no more than awkward imitations of religious life, not to be a trifle sceptical about these demands, but what a loss it would be for the Christian community if vocations like these were entirely excluded. In any case, it seems likely that had the law of the Church left the third orders free to follow the course of their evolution, they would have given birth to much more flexible and diversified forms of religious life.[3] However, it is not my task to re-write history.

With my colleague, Jean Isaac,[4] I very much wonder whether, for the renewal of religious life, it might not prove necessary to explore as yet untried paths. If, as I have said, the renewal of the Church depends on a rediscovery of the presence and role of the Spirit, it is inevitable that we should feel constrained to pay greater attention to the variety of charisms, graces and missions which constitute the ecclesial community. Certain charismatics have, in the past, given birth to real spiritual families where, in principle, there are to be found all who, whatever their state of life, share the same evangelical insights as the founder. Thus, St Dominic, both during his lifetime and after his death,

[2] The rule of the Dominican lay fraternities, promulgated by the supreme authority of the Order, the General Chapter of the Friars, offers lay people who have this vocation the possibility of living the evangelical counsels in the context of the three vows.

[3] It was the Council of Trent, for example, which obliged sisters of the third order to live, like all religious under solemn vows, in strict enclosure. And the life-style of apostolic congregations of the regular third order, which were founded for the most part in the nineteenth century in the wake of the ancient monasteries remained, for a long time, marked by its monastic roots.

[4] J. Isaac, "Voeux de religion, vie commune et familles spirituelles", in *Forma Gregis*, I (1973).

founded a great family, comprising within its institutional framework preaching friars, contemplative nuns, sisters in apostolic congregations and members of lay fraternities or secular institutes.[5]

Unfortunately, both in the Order of Preachers and elsewhere, membership of the spiritual family was too often understood in terms of a hierarchy of social classes, controlled from the top by the male, clerical branch, but without any effective collaboration —which would obviously vary according to the form and mode of membership—to a common end. If this is so, then surely the future will depend, in the first place, on the renewal of these spiritual families which will strive to recapture the special grace and mission of their founder. Jean Isaac writes that in each of these spiritual families "it is to be hoped that there will be room for people of widely varying circumstances. Men and women, married people or celibates, clergy and laity, contemplative or missionary spirits, philosophers or pragmatists, listeners or doers, let all be accepted on an absolutely equal footing, provided only they enjoy the same call, and the future would change."[6]

In this enlarged perspective, the commitment made in religious families at the outset would be the same for all. The only necessary *a priori* requirement would be complete self-donation to God— and therefore donation for life—in the religious family to which the Holy Spirit had led one. After that it would follow that within this family some would hear the call of Christ to the threefold paradoxical renunciations which he himself was the first to make by his triple stand during the temptation in the desert, and would set themselves up in apposition to their brothers and sisters, without, however, isolating themselves from them.[7] Openness to the promptings of the Spirit should surely make us look forward to Utopias of this kind.

Whatever happens, this first observation will have enabled us to verify experimentally the basic insight of Vatican II as expressed in the ecclesiology of the Constitution *Lumen Gentium* on the Church, concerning religious life, namely that it cannot exist in isolation from the people of God and its unique call to

---

[5] P. Raffin, "La vocation des communautés dominicaines", in *Cahiers Saint-Dominique*, 130 (1972), p. 507.

[6] J. Isaac, *op. cit.*, p. 46.   [7] J. Isaac, *op. cit.*, p. 53.

holiness, and that it will never be renewed unless it shares in the spiritual revival of the whole Christian community which might even give birth to new forms of religious life.

II. THE RENEWAL OF RELIGIOUS LIFE IS MANIFESTED BY A SPIRITUAL AWAKENING

Since Vatican II, religious communities—contemplative or apostolic—have found inspiration for their renewal by taking part in the search for God with the Christian community as a whole, and by sustaining an awareness of its spiritual aspirations.

For my own part, I could illustrate the truth of this statement from the experience of several of these communities, male and female. I mention only that of the Fraternities of Bethlehem, a contemplative group founded in France in 1951.[8] Wishing to find a way of sharing the monastic vocation with lay people, the foundress has created a fraternity which already to date numbers more than sixty members, divided into communities of prayer and silence which set out to welcome all who are searching for God, whatever their circumstances. And so, at the heart of the forest of Fontainebleau or of the industrial suburbs of Paris, in the solitude of the Alps or the hubbub of the Latin Quarter in Paris, wherever they find themselves, the sisters try to be one family among others, in which the paradox of prayer, poverty and fraternal love is lived out in such a way that lay people from all walks of life can belong to it as if it were their own: the family of God. In fact groups of young people or adults meet with the sisters and are initiated into the practice of meditation, adoration, self-examination and discovery of the Christ of the gospels in a more living way. In addition to this, teams of lay people—celibate and married, professional and non-professional, young and not so young—have come together round the fraternities of Bethlehem. They share the monastic life during the weekends or in time of retreat, and manage the material affairs of Bethlehem in collaboration with the sisters. Their purpose is to provide lay reception centres, open to all like the fraternities themselves.

[8] G. Minaberry, "Opération porte ouverte de contemplatives", in *Journal des communautés*, 44 (1970), p. 6.

A similar phenomenon is to be found among religious in the United States, to which the name "houses of prayer" has been given. Bernard Häring describes the movement thus: "It concerns about sixty religious congregations, all of them involved in the hospital services, in social work or in education. They are anxious to find the style of prayer best suited to Christians in professional life, and above all to the younger generation. Their specific aim is to bridge the gulf that separates prayer from life. Many congregations have set up permanent 'houses of prayer' in which a relatively small group of sisters, gifted with special charisms, is responsible for guaranteeing an atmosphere of prayer and charity. These 'houses of prayer' are all alike, and they are none of them structured on the basis of the long-established traditions inspired by the life-style of cloistered religious.

"They have set out courageously in search of their own style, in order to become communities of prayer, where silence blends naturally with attempts to create new forms of community prayer. . . . The 'house of prayer' has neither grille nor surrounding walls. It could be called an institution, but only once it is recognized that its characteristics are openness, flexibility and variety of forms. It is a school of prayer where one seeks to understand the inner reality of things. In a 'house of prayer' the underlying assumption is that to live is to experiment. Prayer always reveals man in his pilgrim condition.

"The various 'houses of prayer' are in contact with one another. In Detroit they run an information centre, since there is a desire to share experiences. Alongside the permanent 'house of prayer', and with a view to bringing out its significance, new forms of retreat have been devised. In 1970 and again in 1971, in the United States alone, a hundred and fifty groups of religious, joined by lay people and several groups of priests, came together for periods of six to eight weeks. These groups, ranging in size from five to fifteen persons, searched together for a way of prayer suited to our times, and renewed their life of prayer in a common endeavour, always bearing in mind their apostolate and the needs of the world."[9]

[9] B. Häring, *Les chances de la prière* (Paris, 1972), pp. 23-5. The author, a German Redemptorist, is considered to have been one of the initiators of the "houses of prayer" movement in 1969. Abundant documentation

This second point, too, enables one to estimate just how far religious life is actually caught up in the life of the people of God, and the role it can play as a leaven—when it really is animated by the Spirit of God and sensitive to what is as yet only tentatively expressed—in fostering charity and restoring to faith its enthusiasm and its language. It is significant that in a Church (and a world) where a new sense of brotherhood is gradually emerging, religious communities can offer meeting places not only in order to preach it, but also to share it, and that at the same time the renewal of the communities themselves depends so completely on their readiness to share the gift of the Spirit which they have received.

III. Renewal in the Spirit

This is to be the title of the new book by P.-R. Régamey, the French Dominican, the last volume of a trilogy devoted to a study of religious life.[10] Père Régamey is one of those who, with every justification, have insisted on the urgent need for authentic spiritual renewal in religious institutes,[11] a renewal which, as we noted, has not yet sufficiently penetrated their post-conciliar *aggiornamento*.

But where are religious to find the impulse of the Spirit, if not at the heart of the Church and the world as they attend with particular vigilance to the needs and appeals of both? Through the upheavals which have affected the old familiar world and through awkward, clumsy turns of phrase, we can glimpse the emergence of a new world in search of brotherhood and freedom. Is it not precisely the vocation of the Church to isolate from among these many calls the authentic voice of the Spirit, to reveal the meaning of the search and give it a name?

---

concerning the movement may be found in the brochure "Exploring Inner Space" (obtainable from Sr Ann Chester, Clearing Centre for House of Prayer Movement, 610 W. Elm Avenue, Monroe, Michigan, 48161 U.S.A.).

[10] P.-R. Régamey, *Redécouvrir la vie religieuse*: I *L'exigence de Dieu* (Paris, 1969); II *La voix de Dieu dans les voix du temps* (Paris, 1973); III *La rénovation dans l'Esprit*, to be published later.

[11] P.-R. Régamey, "La vie religieuse, vie 'pneumatique'", in *Vie Consacrée*, 4 (1969), p. 193.

It is beyond dispute that only by trying to establish new forms of community and by creating the favourable conditions in which each believer can develop his own charisms—and these are the very ways that the Spirit is pointing out to it from all sides—will the Church be able to pass on the Good News to the men of today. It is striking that the great founders—charismatics *par excellence*—faithfully followed up those calls of their age of which they had become aware through a gift of the Spirit and this was, without doubt, the reason for their singular and effective influence. And it is by rediscovering *today*, removed from the context of the age that watched them emerge, the grace and mission of their founder, that spiritual families will also rediscover their inspiration, their unity and their effectiveness. It involves something much more than merely superficial adaptation, equivalent to the plastering over of a cracked façade.

If, faced with the demands and calls of the contemporary Church and world, a spiritual family can no longer experience the same sense of shock as the founder, it will inevitably weaken spiritually—and after that what is the point of clinging to existence? It may also happen that the needs which called a particular spiritual family into existence have disappeared, in which case the desire to preserve the institution at all costs becomes mere archaism. But it may equally happen that the new needs are as yet unsatisfied, and must hasten the birth of new families to undertake as yet untried commitments and projects. The real fidelity of religious institutes cannot, therefore, be expressed by mere repetition of yesterday's patterns but by creative awareness, in the Spirit, of the here and now. This is what the accumulated evidence mentioned so far has to teach us. It is by carrying out to the full the *actual* demands of faith that lay people are inspired to undertake forms of self-commitment similar to those to be found in the religious life, but on the other hand, it is by endeavouring to respond to the deepest appeals of their age that religious communities experience a renewal of vigour.

The source of an institute's renewal—and it is on this that the five criteria mentioned in *Perfectae Caritatis* concentrate—will not be found in some project symbolized by a model or rationalized by a definition, but in that upheaval, that experience of being shaken to the core, shared indeed with the founder, but in confrontation with today's realities. This shows how essential it is to begin by listening for a long time to the Spirit. In the absense of this patient listening and this inspiration, one will catch hold of nothing but ephemeral and uninspiring realities.

So it is this creative docility to the promptings of the Spirit which will make of the Church a veritable symphony of charisms, all directed towards service of the community. In this charismatic symphony every spiritual family is then urged to play its part, and within each one the originality of each state of life—the religious life being one—has the right to be recognized. Religious life, as a charismatic state, writes P. Jacquemont, will be "a way of organizing life so as to call attention to the relative value of the 'world' in comparison with the urgency of the coming of the kingdom. The particular charism of the religious life seems to be its stress on the awareness, awakened by the Spirit, that the kingdom is both an imminent gift of God, since he is already at the door, and a free gift of God, since we cannot force the door open. The charism of religious life—and in this it differs from marriage—is to interpret the coming of the kingdom as something to be awaited and welcomed, and to enshrine that interpretation in a state of life capable of revealing it."[12]

The spiritual renewal of religious life must clearly be accompanied by a renewed theology of religious life, which will present it as but one charism among the many charisms of the Church. The Holy Spirit's presence is recognized, not as something haphazard, but as integral to the very structure of renewal, in the return to the sources and the lasting reform of religious life; and so it all becomes a question not so much of spiritual awakening but of placing the Spirit at the centre once more. A theology of religious life cannot be neutral. When religious life is presented as a charismatic gift, there is implied an invitation to enduring contact with the sources, which nevertheless remains open to the promptings of the Spirit and conscious of the fact that he allows for variety in the way the charism is expressed.

[12] P. Jacquemont, "Charismes et état de vie. Vie conjugale et vie religieuse", in *Forma Gregis*, 4 (1972), p. 15.

We must be careful not to reduce this spiritual revival to mere renewal of fervour in cosy little communities, and careful, too, not to separate the spiritual renewal of religious life from the renewal of the Church. The first is born of the second, and its fruits must be shared with the whole Church.

Translated by Sarah Fawcett

Biographical Notes

ENZO BIANCHI was born in 1943 at Castel Boglione in the Monferrato (Italy). After completing his studies in economics at Turin University, he went to the village of Bose to initiate a cenobitic community of many confessions committed to the study of the Bible. He is the leader of that community. His published works include many liturgical texts in *Preghiera per la communità—breviario ecumenico per l'anno liturgico—ufficio di Bose* (Brescia, 1971); a rhythmical and choral version of the Psalms (Brescia, 1971); *Il Corvo di Elia*, an introduction to prayer (Turin, 1972); *Ritorno alle fonti della vita religiosa*, in preparation; *Lectio divina dell' Evangelo di Marco* (Brescia, 1973); articles in *Servitium* and *Il Gallo*, of which he is an editor.

SEGUNDO GALILEA was born in Santiago (Chile) in 1928 and was ordained priest in 1956. From 1963 onwards, he collaborated in the Pastoral Section of CELAM, the Episcopal Council of Latin America, first in Mexico, then in Ecuador. At present, he is the director of the Pastoral Institute of Latin America (IPLA), which is part of CELAM. His publications include *Hacia una Pastoral Vernácula* (1964); *Para una Pastoral Latinoamericana* (1968); *Reflexiones sobre la Evangelización* (1969); *A los Pobres se anuncia el Evangelio?* (1971); *Contemplación y Apostolado* (1972); *Espiritualidad de la Liberación* (1973). He has also written many articles on pastoral questions in Latin America.

DONALD GELPI, S.J., is professor of dogmatic and historical theology at the Jesuit School of Theology at Berkeley. He is also co-director of the Berkeley Institute for Spirituality and Worship. From 1969 to 1970, he was assistant professor of philosophy and religious studies at Loyola University in New Orleans. He received his doctorate in American philosophy from Fordham University in 1970. He holds graduate degrees in philosophy and theology from St Louis University. From 1961 to 1963, he did theological studies at the Collège St Albert in Louvain. He is the author of *Life and Light: A Guide to the Theology of Karl Rahner*; *Functional Asceticism: A Guideline for American Religious*; *Discerning the Spirit: Foundations and Futures of Religious Life*; *Pentecostalism: A Theological Viewpoint*; *Pentecostal Piety*.

CLAUDE GÉREST, a Dominican, was born at Saint-Étienne (France) in February 1921. He studied history at Lyons and theology at the Dominican centre at St Alban-Leyss. He also studied at the Institut d'Histoire européenne at Mainz under Professor Lortz. He teaches at the seminaries of Lyons and Viviers, is an assistant lecturer at the Catholic faculty at the University of Lyons and is on the staff at the Ecumenical Centre St Irenée. He is a contributor to *Lumière et Vie*.

DANIÈLE HERVIEU-LÉGER was born on 3 February 1947 in Paris. She has a diploma from the Institut d'Études politiques, Paris, is a licentiate in law and a doctor of sociology. She lectures at the Collège Coopératif (École pratique des Hautes Études) and at the Institut d'Études sociales, Paris. She has done research work in the sociology of religion on the political and religious views of Catholic students in France and on the development of Catholic grass-roots communities. At present, she is studying various aspects of the recent anti-institutional movement in the West. Her publications include "De la mission à la protestation", in *L'Évolution des étudiants chrétiens en France (1965–1970)* (Paris,/ 1973); "L'Idéologie politico-religieuse des groupes informels d'étudiants: essai d'interprétation", in *Les Groupes Informels dans l'Église* (Strasbourg, 1971); "Systèmes de représentations religieuses et politiques dans un groupe d'étudiants catholiques", in *Psychologie Sociale et Religion* (Paris, 1972); "Le développement des communautés de base et leur contexte religieux en France", in *Archives Internationales de Sociologie de la Coopération et du Développement*, No. 31 (Jan.–June 1972). She has also contributed articles to the reviews *Esprit, Projet, Lumière et Vie, La Maison-Dieu*, etc.

ROLAND MURPHY, born on 19 July 1917, in Chicago, is an American Carmelite and a member of the editorial board of *Concilium*. He is professor of Old Testament studies at the Duke University Divinity School in Durham and is the author of several articles and books dealing with the Old Testament.

PIERRE RAFFIN was born in 1938 in Nancy (France), became a Dominican in 1956 and was ordained priest in 1964. He studied philosophy and theology at the Saulchoir and at the Institut Catholique at Toulouse. From 1968 until 1971, he was master of the Dominican students at the Saulchoir. Since January 1972, he has been religious assistant to the lay Dominican fraternities in France. He has contributed to various dictionaries and reviews and is counsellor to several lay groups and religious communities.

GÜNTER REMMERT was born in Fulda (West Germany) in 1947. A Jesuit, he studied philosophy in Pullbach near Munich and in Berlin and is at present studying theology in Frankfurt. He has published articles on the charismatic movements in various journals.

JOHN-DAVID ROBINSON was born in Utah in 1930 on the feast of the Beheading of St John the Baptist, a fact discovered after a Stoic childhood and Buddhist teens upon seeking baptism into Christ in the Roman Catholic Church at 20. Winner of Vogue's Prix de Paris at 16, he also studied at the Arts Students' League School in New York. Philosophy studies in the great books programme, St John's College, Annapolis, Md., and the University of Utah; theology and church history at Harvard; research in Early Christian and Byzantine archaeology and iconography at Princeton. His publications include the award winning audio-visual catechesis "Baptism and the New Creation". He is a fellow and the programme director of the Centre for Spiritual Studies, a service agency for inter-religious activities. He directed the Mount Saviour Symposium on spiritualities in world religions.

FERNANDO URBINA is a diocesan priest in Madrid. Born in 1923, in Murcia, Spain, he studied at the seminary in Madrid and at the faculty of theology at Granada. He has been in the parish ministry, has worked as a chaplain and has been the superior of the Hispano-American Seminary and the seminary in Madrid. At present, he teaches pastoral theology at the faculty of theology of Granada and Comillas (Madrid).

JUAN MARTIN VELASCO was born on 8 March 1934 at Santa Cruz del Valle (Ávila) and was ordained priest in Madrid. He studied philosophy at the Catholic University of Louvain, where he obtained a doctorate in 1960. From 1962 until 1970, he taught at the seminary in Madrid. At present, he teaches philosophy of religion and phenomenology at the Pontifical University of Salamanca and is the director of the Institute of Advanced Pastoral Studies at Madrid. His most important publications include *Hacia una filosofía de la religión cristiana. La obra de H. Duméry* (1970); "El proceso de secularización desde la perspectiva de la fenomenología religiosa", *Fe e y nueva sensibilidad histórica* (1972); "El desarrollo de un logos interno a la religión", *Convicción de fe y crítica racional* (1972); *Fenomenología de la religión* (1973).